HOMEDADDY

Little White Lies & Other Tales from the Crib

TODD PINSKY

cartoons by
JERRY DOLEZAL

For Janet,
Keep laughing,
while it is still legal.
Todd Pinsky

PUSH
PULL
PRESS

SANTA CRUZ, CALIFORNIA
www.pushpullpress.com

For information on Homedaddy, inquiries about the Homedaddy weekly column, or to schedule Todd Pinsky to speak at an event, contact:
Push Pull Press
Tel: (888) 909-7874
Fax: (831) 466-0208
E-Mail: marketing@pushpullpress.com
Internet: www.pushpullpress.com

06 05 04 03 02   6 5 4 3 2

Pinsky, Todd
   Homedaddy / Todd Pinsky.—1st. ed.
   ISBN 0-9728244-0-5
      1. Humor—United States.   2. Parenting—United States

Library of Congress Cataloging-in-Publication control #2003101594.

Book Design by Julia Pinsky
Cartoons by Jerry Dolezal
Typefaces: Mrs. Eaves & Bembo

To my family.

Special thanks to Michael Chihak for encouraging the Homedaddy column and running it in his newspaper; and to Dave Barry for his vote of confidence and for proving all of my teachers wrong (you can *too* crack wise for a living).

CONTENTS

Foreword

During my existence B.C. (Before Children), I never felt especially attached to any of my numerous jobs, and it wasn't until I became a full-time dad that I ever felt I'd found the right line of work. Many people are curious about how it transpired. Was it something I had always dreamed of, or did I stumble into it; and what on earth gave me the idea that I might be qualified? Did I study at a special training facility, or did I just answer an ad on the inside of a matchbook?

Truthfully, we never planned it this way. At the time Julia, my wife, got pregnant, she was Creative Services Manager for a high-tech company, and I was production manager at a small-town TV station. The working assumption was that after the baby was born, we'd act like other dual-income yuppies and hire full-time childcare. Here's what we discovered: Just because you work so much you stagger around like zombies doesn't mean you can afford a nanny.

We watched with mild disbelief as our accountant drew pictures to prove that my salary, minus taxes, car expense and aspirin, would barely be enough to hire a total stranger to raise our child. That got us wondering: Could we even afford to keep two jobs? Unlike me, Julia really enjoyed her work, and since she just so happened to earn twice as much, it was my job at the TV station that conveniently went on the block.

My job! It could have been fun, in a wacky sort of way, producing unintentionally silly car lot commercials featuring pompous dealers in bad toupees bungling their way through the insipid sales pitch. It was amusing at first, that is until our out-of-state Goliath Parent Corporation, following industry trends, began imposing respectable corporate culture on us rubes. Before you could say "raise the bar", "be proactive", and "step up to the plate," they were distributing shiny new employee handbooks, mounting framed mission statements on the restroom walls, making us be accountable… basically taking all the fun out of everything.

Having already reached the point of job burnout, the prospect of full-time parenthood seemed like a perfect solution for me. I no longer had to fear the day that some bit of corporate doublespeak would finally drive me around the bend, and that I'd barge onto the set of the local news to resign in spectacular fashion, waving a beaker of gin and ranting about George Orwell.

I composed a resignation letter so sappy you could stick a bucket under it and make syrup. "With mixed emotions blah blah blah measure of regret blah blah blah tender my resignation blah blah blah…" Then I delicately shoveled on a few finishing touches about how wonderful the job had been, how proud and thankful I felt, and how the company had always treated me like family.

I didn't see the point in mentioning that my family included people who hadn't spoken to each other in years.

Everything went smooth as silk. Instead of being escorted off the premises by security guards, I enjoyed a hero's farewell. Many people felt that sacrificing my "career" in order to serve my family was a noble act. Who was I to burst their bubble? Hell, I was looking forward to an ironclad excuse to hang out in my underwear and watch cartoons until 2 PM. Of course, it didn't work out exactly like that, but… well, you'll hear all about it.

NEWBORN TIPS

Four months ago, my wife, Julia gave birth to our first child Emma Louise. Since I now know everything there is to know about birth 'n babies, I am qualified to clear up any confusion you may have regarding this complex process. Here are a few tidbits of essential information to get you off to the right start with your newborn.

Bonding. This is a continuation of the mother–child relationship that began in the womb. However, since the baby is now a distinctly separate physical entity, some people feel the child should be "bonded" before the relationship is allowed to continue. Many parents feel that as soon as the bond is paid and their child is issued a bond number, they will know their new child is reliable. If a bond cannot be secured at the hospital you may wish to call a bondsman. In any case, there is little evidence that a lack of early bonding is detrimental, and many pediatricians downplay the importance of bonding on the grounds that the average newborn is not a flight risk.

Calming Your Baby. You new fathers out there might have noticed that babies like motion, but did you know that it's not just any old movement that can prevent the infant's heartbreaking squall? Recent studies have shown that the inner ear mechanisms of most babies are so sensitive that they are actually able to tell the difference between useful and useless motion. Most babies, like Emma, prefer useless motion. As long as I'm shuffling along aimlessly or bobbing pointlessly from foot to foot everything's just fine, but if I lean over to read something or to place a dish in the sink, she goes off like a car alarm. She requires my full attention. No multi-tasking.

Diapers. Just like with everything else, you've got some decisions to make regarding your baby's diapers. You can use cloth diapers or disposables. The cloth ones are specially designed and are about as absorbent as porcelain. Nowadays you can get them with built-in plastic snaps, but if adventure's your game go ahead and use pins. Disposable diapers work so well that the only way you know they need changing is when your child is suddenly too heavy to lift. At least you get the chance to do your patriotic duty and support the landfill industry. Convenience is what it's about, anyway. Who wants to wash diapers? We got lucky and received a few months worth of diaper service as a gift. If you're nostalgic you can always wash them yourself. If you're really nostalgic you can go smash two hydrogen atoms together and make your own water first.

Above all, allow yourself to fall in love with your baby. Do not be alarmed if he looks more like Babe Ruth or Alfred Hitchcock than you or your mate. You are still in a state of shock from the birth experience. Soon your body will manufacture the hormones that cause you to suddenly recognize cuteness in anyone, and in no time at all you'll be able to look at a photo of Babe Ruth and say, "Awww, no wonder they called him 'Babe.'"

BJORN IN THE USA

If you were one of the people who saw me walking down the street the other day with the dog and the baby, let me explain. First of all, it is hard enough controlling a hundred pound Labrador with a brain the size of a walnut, let alone while carrying an infant child in one of those yuppie strap-on gadgets that holds the kid snug against your chest. You've seen these things, they look like prosthetic kangaroo pouches. Only good taste and the threat of legal action stops me from mentioning them by their brand name. They are state-of-the-art Scandinavian design, and everyone knows that the Scandinavians know more than anyone about raising children, which is why they are the world's leading exporter of au pairs.

These units are painstakingly engineered to allow the hardworking parent to "wear" the child during the day while doing simple tasks, and to evenly distribute the child's weight through the shoulder straps and, in my case, directly onto the spine at the L5 vertebra which eventually causes tingling and numbness in the legs. It can be used in the "face-out" configuration, which allows the Little One to enjoy an unobstructed view of the world

while experiencing the unique sensation of being duct-taped to your chest (essential for building self esteem), or the "face-in" mode, which uses the natural absorbency of your shirt to protect the sidewalk from those pesky little barf stains.

As a Homedaddy it is my duty to correct any imbalances in our household such as, for example, a shortage of plastic pants to wrap around our politically-correct cloth diapers. Yes, that's right, we've decided to participate a little less in the national pastime of Making The Landfill Overflow by using cloth diapers specially handmade by hippie moms in a teepee on an all-organic commune during the summer solstice... diapers made using an ancient sacred technique which gives them the absorbency of masonite. Therefore it is necessary to use plastic pants made from chemicals developed by DuPont in order to catch the runoff. And since our baby, Emma, grows so fast you can hear her creaking if you listen closely, it is not unusual to discover, in any given moment, that none of her plastic pants will fit.

No problem, Homedaddy to the rescue; we'll strap on the prosthetic kangaroo pouch and walk downtown to get some new plastic pants. Heck, it's a nice day, let's take Wilson for a walk while we're at it. Wilson is, of course, the aforementioned hundred-pound Labrador.

OK, maybe it wasn't such a nice day, maybe it was something like a jillion degrees, and I didn't really walk the dog so much as get dragged along in his wake. But with the sun at our backs I was able to keep Emma shaded and before you knew it she was fast asleep and all I had to worry about was the dog ripping my arm out of its socket like a turkey drumstick.

The real trouble started on the return trip. Emma was finished with her nap and wanted to be home. We still had a mile or so to go and the sun was right in our faces. I'd recently read a scary article in a parenting magazine that said if you let your baby get sunburned she'll get to be sixteen and wreck your car, so I was trying to keep her hat pulled down low over her eyes, which only made her hotter and angrier. When she started protesting in earnest I started to panic and put the power walk into gear. I was only trying to get home on the double, but to my relief, the increased pace and bumpier ride calmed Emma right down.

A painful moment later I realized that the action of her little legs swinging back and forth was causing her heels to come into solid contact with a part of my anatomy generally not known for its ability to effectively absorb impact. I immediately slowed my gait enough to make her legs swing a little less...just enough to correct the previous condition, but for Emma, the decrease of urgency in my homeward motion was a big negative. The slower I walked, the more she cried.

Clearly, I had to make some adjustments. I tried walking with my hands placed protectively over my groin, but the shopping bag on one wrist and Wilson's leash on the other rendered this approach impractical. Besides, people were staring. I slowed down to think, but Emma's wail did nothing to reassure the troubled onlookers. I sped up again, this time trying to customize my walk. I achieved some success by thrusting my chest forward every other step, which did alter the arc of her dangerous leg-swing path, but which also made me appear to be strutting like a peacock. Now more people were staring, and some began pointing. Again I resumed a normal gait, and again, the baby started yelling. I finally arrived at the solution: a nifty little reverse pelvic thrust step; sort of a Groucho Marx-meets-Elvis-on-Viagra. People were still staring and pointing but at least Emma was satisfied and I was making good time.

So if you were one of those people who saw me out walking the other day, please, don't worry, everything's fine. The baby was in no danger. That strange man was her father and he is not criminally insane. A little adjustment on the straps of his Scandinavian kangaroo prosthetic ought to take care of everything.

S'NOT FOR EVERYONE

Sooner or later the honeymoon is over, and your sweet baby, your healthy, content, sound-sleeping angel, who has been functioning quite well up till now as a Bliss Delivery System, will finally succumb to her first cold and its accompanying Jeckyl-and-Hyde personality shift. The early warning signs: refusal to eat, sit up, lie down, stay awake, go to sleep, stay indoors, go outdoors, be held or be put down. Heed these danger signals or not, your baby is about to show you some new tricks, including the bubbly wheeze, the fever, the chain saw cough, and oh, did I mention the snot? Copious amounts of it; thick as roofing tar.

But what to do? Our experience with Emma up to this point had been so warm and fuzzy it makes the Teletubbies seem abusive, but suddenly, there we were, in the middle of the night scrambling around in the dark like Keystone Kops while Emma howled curses which, if translated from the original Infant tongue, would be unprintable. As the 6 AM wake-up call drew near, we realized for the first time how easy we've had it. Our respect for parents with "special needs" children was distilled to pure awe.

There is nothing so pathetic as panicked yuppies. We hauled out the baby-owner's manual, an encyclopedia-sized book whose cover features a gratuitous close-up of a Professional Model baby. The author, a frizzy-haired, lab-coated Child Development Specialist, looks like a man who could scare the rubber pants off a baby just by sticking his head into the room. He devotes a long chapter to colds, their symptoms and causes, and mainly about how you can't do anything to cure them. Since babies can't blow their own noses, it is necessary to — and this certainly caught our attention — suck the snot out of their noses for them.

This was a curious bit of information to ponder in the middle of the night, and it started a brief and confused argument over who would do the dirty work. Neither of us wanted to set a precedent. Imagine my relief at dawn as I re-read the chapter in better light and realized that this task is accomplished with a little rubber bulb called a "snot sucker," or in mixed company, an "aspirator." This was more like it... I had feared something more like a snakebite scenario.

With much relief I packed Emma down to the drug store (it used to be "Thrifty" before being taken over by the "Kant Spel" corporation) to get properly outfitted. Once home and ready to get down to business, I made another startling discovery: Sick babies don't really want to be pinned down in a headlock while some evil alien scientist in a cheap rubber Daddy mask attempts to use an unfamiliar object with a pointed tip to suck their brains out via their sinuses. Jeez, who would have figured they'd have a problem with that? Certainly not the brainiac who "wrote the book" on baby snot.

He was right about one thing, though. You can't make the cold go away. What you can do, in the meantime, is make numerous midnight runs to the drugstore and spend lots of money in efforts to feel helpful. Aspirators, thermometers, electrolyte solutions, humidifiers, vaporizers... parting with money always makes you feel as though you're doing all you can.

But nothing really helps, and the nights start to blend together. You can't lay 'em down, they're too congested, and no matter how exhausted they are or how soundly they fall asleep, they're going to wake up gurgling and hacking in ten minutes. Your only hope is to try to keep the baby upright and hope she can fall asleep that way. It's a good plan except that you must be awake all night to do it. What the heck, you're not going to get any sleep anyway. It's a long-shot. You bounce, dance shuffle around, try the rocking chair... just as you twist into an impossible position you hear one of those tiny little baby snores. Ahh, relief. Just one slight move to straighten your spine, and... oops, back to the dance floor.

Another aspect to your child's cold which bears mentioning is that you and your spouse will also get sick, although not till you've stayed awake with the baby for a couple of nights. Sleep deprivation serves the dual purpose of weakening your immune system while softening your brain, so you won't see it coming till it's too late. You'll just have a bizarre dream where lab-coated thugs beat you with rubber bulbs, throw you down a flight of stairs, and inject Krazy Glue up your nose and into both ears. Upon arising you will find, to your dismay, that it was not a dream at all... they even left their rubber bulb behind.

THE FOUR SECOND WINDOW

When your baby is first born you are thrust into a state of over-the-top bliss which is best exemplified by an utterly saccharine message on your answering machine, done in your best Mr. Rogers tone of voice: "Hi everyone... you have reached the home of Sam, Paula... and our new little special guest star Brittany... (tee hee hee)... we can't come to the phone now 'cause we're in dreamland..." You've been lulled into believing that the rest of your life will proceed in a state of pure happiness, and that eleven minutes of sleep per week is plenty.

Eventually you will be forced to re-engage with the outside world, at which time reality will reappear in the form of parking tickets, fleas, leaking roofs, bad haircuts, telemarketers, and local television commercials. The negativity generated by these experiences allows the awareness of your fatigue to get a foothold, and when the insides of your eyelids feel like sandpaper and you crave three or four days of uninterrupted sleep, you start to get protective of your spare time.

Although it is common to experience sudden waves of hostility towards anything which threatens to disturb your momentary and hard-earned peace of mind, you must remember that babies are emotional sponges; they are far too fragile to withstand exposure to any negative outbursts. Therefore, in order to prevent Permanent Emotional Scarring (also known as "growing up") you must wear the Happy Face™ and make the Happy Cooing Sound™ in order to fool the little one into thinking that all is well in the world. Ha ha ha, children are so gullible.

After a few short months you'll have more to worry about than your tone of voice and facial expressions, since your baby will have entered that precious and lovable stage where everything goes into the mouth. Any object which is not actually bolted to some sort of foundation is a choking hazard for infants and toddlers. Never let your guard down, even during the early months, since many infants exhibit what is known as "Magnetic Trachea Syndrome," a condition where all objects in a room which are smaller than a forklift are magnetically attracted toward the child's windpipe. Many new parents have had the confusing experience of laying Baby down for a nap in a clean bed and returning to find the pillow surrounded by car keys, guitar picks, lipsticks, pennies, golf tees, cough lozenges, and Monopoly houses. This is often mistaken for paranormal activity by parents who watch too much television.

When your baby is old enough to sit up without mechanical assistance you may be tempted to plunk him down on the floor while attempting to perform some household task. You may have even worked out a simple routine such as taking the kitchen trash bag out to the can, a move which you have timed out to exactly seven seconds. The moment Baby turns his head away, you can grab the trash, run outside, throw it in the can, and run back inside to a proper viewing angle before he's had time to plug in the Cuisinart. Remember, as playthings go, high-speed rotating knives are politically incorrect at best, so don't loaf on your way back into the house.

Babies are very resourceful when motivated, and are very fast learners. If you have the trash dash timed out to seven seconds, he'll review his process and find a way to eliminate unnecessary steps which will then enable him to activate the Cuisinart in six seconds.

Exhaustive research at Homedaddy™ Labs has established a four second window, now known as "The Four Second Window" and recognized as the industry standard, during which you can safely look away from your baby. This is the average amount of time needed for Baby to stick the top half of a bowling trophy down his throat, or in the case of an extremely precocious child, to burn your entire house to the ground. Some parents have "trained" Baby to go for slightly longer stretches of time, and one reader claims to achieve spans of up to eleven seconds with the use of simple restraining straps. We at Homedaddy Inc.™ do not endorse this technique, except perhaps on the parent.

There is no substitute for constant vigilance. You may have served as a babysitter sometime in your past, but that probably meant acting as referee for a knock-down-drag-out Monopoly grudge match between the neighbor's pre-teens. Infants are another story.

You can't even have a decent game of Monopoly with an infant. Babies do not have the worldly experience to deal with complex situations and will usually attempt a life-threatening maneuver such as inhaling a hotel or purchasing Water Works.

Speaking of Monopoly, did you know that it is a sure-fire cure for Baby's fever when she gets sick? Here's how it works: At the first hint of a fever (non-stop continuous wailing from 2 to 6 AM with no inhale is one telltale sign), start up a friendly game of Monopoly. By the time the game is over, Baby will not only be finished with her fever, she'll be finished with grad school. The best part of this plan is that if you lose, you can throw a tantrum, since she'll be old enough to handle it.

SLEEPING LIKE A BABY

Emma's naps rule my life. I am no longer on the same clock as the rest of my time zone, or the rest of the civilized world for that matter. I now operate on Pacific Nap Time. Instead of AM and PM, my day is broken down into BN, DN, and AN, which stand for Before Nap, During Nap, and After Nap, respectively. All my scheduling now occurs within this context.

Emma's naps are the fundamental units of any remaining sanity in our household, and therefore receive the highest possible priority. A missed nap is a Red Alert situation. All hands on deck. There is such a thing as a baby who is too tired to go to sleep, and if you have never been around one, you don't want to know about it.

Lulling Emma to sleep, putting her down, and getting her up again afterwards... the whole nap culture is the driving force which shapes my days. Emma normally takes two naps a day; one in the morning and one in the afternoon. But at this point it gets complicated. The naps range from 15 minutes to three hours in length and can strike at any time. You don't want to go out on errands with a sleepy baby; getting her in and out of the car seat is very disruptive. I don't even try it anymore. Nowadays, if I miscalculate her Awareness Cycle and she nods off a block from the house I will scrub the mission and resort to Plan B, which involves dishes or laundry, or Plan C, which involves lunch.

You can't overestimate the importance of your baby's naps. Their rapidly growing little bodies need the downtime to recover from the day's radical expenditure of energy, and you need a few minutes to yourself to rest, meditate, or perhaps fold forty pounds of laundry. Sometimes you will just need this time to read something besides *Pat The Bunny*, which may be a timeless piece of children's literature, but is probably better known for its fake bunny-fur insert on page four than for its grindingly predictable plot and insipid dialogue.

A sleepy baby is a powder keg, the only notable difference being that it is OK to jiggle a sleepy baby. Here at Homedaddy Inc.™, our research team has developed several proprietary techniques for shepherding the groggy infant into Dreamland. The early favorite was a simple stroller ride with the seat in the reclined position. This was found to be even more efficient over

slightly bumpy terrain. Unfortunately the underlying logic did not translate to related techniques; our early experiments with a car seat, duct tape, and a paint-mixing machine produced disappointing results.

Audio, or sound technique, has been another exciting avenue of nap research. Acting on an anonymous tip, we found that the sound of a hair dryer causes Emma, provided she is in a pre-nap condition, to abandon her current train of thought in favor of a sudden interest in the insides of her eyelids. Normally, it takes only a couple of minutes of this sound to produce sleep. The experts are divided in their theories of why this works. The best explanation is that there is something mind-numbing about the sound of hot air rushing past. We tested this theory by watching C-SPAN and found the results to be conclusive: In all test cases, the subjects were sound asleep in a matter of seconds.

Once your baby is asleep, you've got to put her down without waking her, a process which takes us back to the powder keg analogy: one false move and bingo. A baby can be asleep in your arms so soundly that a slamming door won't cause a twitch, but she'll still jerk suddenly awake at your first hint of a motion towards the bed. Some days it can take so many attempts that the morning nap becomes the afternoon nap by default.

And when you do succeed, you're still not out of the woods. If you wish to do something in another room you must use a so-called baby monitor, which differs from the military issue walkie-talkie primarily in the use of puppies and kittens as a design motif. By using the baby monitor, not only do you free yourself up to move around the house, but you also provide your child with a valuable vocational skill. Research has shown that children who are used to being monitored with an electronic listening device will have an easier time adapting to corporate culture as adults.

Nowadays I just put her on the bed, although in the early months we used a bassinet. Hey, here's a little trivia for you: The bassinet is named for Chief Bassinet of the Nez Perce Indians, whose small but hardy band, although driven to fatigue, built ingenious tree houses to allow the tribe's 500 exhausted children to sleep peacefully, undisturbed and undiscovered by the U.S. Cavalry. Strangely, it was the world of auto racing that chose to recognize this heroic chapter in history by staging a major race each year to commemorate the event... don't tell me you've never heard of the Indian Nap-less 500...

BREAKFAST IN SHORT ORDER

If your wife is out there all the week bringing home the bacon, it is crucial that you, the support system, seize an occasional opportunity to remind her that she is a goddess worthy of great rewards. Here at Homedaddy™ Research Labs we have achieved excellent results with a process called Cooking Saturday Breakfast and Tending the Baby while Mom sleeps in.

Cooking, like many other household tasks, becomes a brand new adventure when attempted with a baby in the crook of your arm. It's tough enough just to cook one-handed, but even worse when your baby gets fussy and does her impression of the Heisman Trophy, planting a wicked stiff-arm to your Adam's apple while driving hard with her legs.

Of course, these and other skills are covered in my exclusive Homedaddy™ series of lectures, seminars, videos, audiocassettes, and encounter weekends. As a special courtesy this week, I present, gratis, the Homedaddy™ Technique for Saturday Morning Gourmet Omelet with Home Fried Potatoes.

Ingredients and supplies:

6 eggs
1 pinch dried herbs
2 small onions
1 tomato
1 handful grated smoked Gouda cheese
1 roasted red pepper
1 fresh jalapeño pepper
1 large potato
1 omelet pan
1 cast iron skillet

1 baby
1 highchair
1 roll aluminum foil
1 clean diaper
1 clean pair plastic pants
1 nursery rhyme video
2 rag dolls
1 teddy bear
1 jar baby food

Hold the baby in your left arm, keeping your hip cocked at a 45-degree angle to help support the weight. With your free hand, wash the potato. Poke holes in the skin with a fork... the potato, not the baby. Wrap the baby securely in aluminum foil to protect from radiation and microwave the spud on high power for 5 minutes. Those of you in a twelve-step program can use Higher power. Remove cooked potato from microwave and set aside. Remove foil from baby. Place baby in highchair and slowly add the first rag doll until calm.

Pre-heat omelet pan over high heat. Chop the onion, tomato, roasted pepper, and jalapeño and set aside. Crack 3 eggs into a bowl and beat with a whisk. When baby cries from the onion fumes, remove her from highchair and run out onto the porch. When baby is calm, hand her to your next-door neighbor, run back into the smoke-filled house, kill the burner under the pan, yank the battery out of the smoke alarm, and crawl back outside. Argue politics with neighbor until smoke clears from house. Return with baby on hip.

When omelet pan is no longer glowing red, use your free hand to sauté the jalapeño pepper and half of the chopped onions in butter till soft. Remove and set aside.

Place baby on living room floor in front of TV set and start nursery rhyme video. Run back to kitchen and preheat cast iron skillet. Running back to living room, remove baby from back of TV set where she is chewing on cables. Introduce the second rag doll, using a high-pitched "silly voice" and a pathetic ventriloquism technique which could only fool a baby. Run back to kitchen.

Slice the cooked potato into small cubes. Drop some butter into the skillet and add the potato and the rest of the onions. Fry over high heat until baby starts to cry in the other room.

Run into living room, knocking over a small bookshelf. Check baby's diaper, run back to the kitchen, reduce heat under the spuds, and then change the diaper. Set baby down on living room floor with teddy bear. Rewind nursery rhyme video and start again. Run back into kitchen and wash your hands.

Preheat omelet pan, add butter, and pour in the eggs. Cook over medium heat until, out of the corner of your eye, you see a planter containing a small ficus tree falling in the next room. Dive headfirst into the room and catch the planter an inch or two from the ground. Pick up baby and return to kitchen. Place baby once again in the highchair. Open the jar of baby food and attempt to feed until baby offers minor resistance. Continue to offer the spoon until she swats it out of your hand. Kneel in front of highchair and when you have her attention, perform a demonstration by feeding yourself a couple of spoonfuls.

When you suddenly remember what you're supposed to be doing, spin around and remove omelet pan from the heat. Scrape the carboniferous eggs out of the pan with a screwdriver and feed to the dog. Put baby in stroller and walk to a supermarket and buy a cheap fry pan. Return home and start over.

Or scrap the whole project, wait for your ever lovin' to wake up, and take the family out for a nice brunch.

CLEANLINESS IS NEXT TO IMPOSSIBLE

Fact: You cannot simultaneously keep a clean house and be an attentive parent. Housekeeping while on baby duty is limited to things you can do with one hand while balancing a squirming 25 pounds with the other. You can't do the really tough cleaning jobs while caring for a baby since these jobs require you to be on your hands and knees in restricted spaces for extended periods of time. Any infant in his right mind will protest, and any parent who hates to scrub toilets and showers will heed.

You'd have to neglect your child to keep your house really clean all the time, but of course I conform to a higher standard. I wouldn't dream of abandoning Emma for that length of time, and believe me it breaks my heart not to be able to spend hours scrubbing the grout between the shower tiles with a toothbrush dipped in bleach. It's just another personal sacrifice I must make.

The real goal of being a new parent is for the child to love you, and little kids don't give a rat's keister about a clean house. Remember when you were a kid? Who were the most popular parents? Not the ones with slipcovers on the sofas, plastic runways bisecting all carpeted areas, and irrational rules about sitting on beds. No, the popular parents were the ones with a nice comfy layer of clutter on everything. I am not saying that a messy house is a prerequisite to good parenting, but I am saying that a meticulously clean house will impress your baby about as much as C-SPAN.

Because I've made this decision of conscience to sacrifice the pleasures of sore knees, dishpan hands, and mystic visions from inhaling disinfectant fumes, we have a cleaning lady come in every few weeks. Her impending visit always prompts a flurry of preliminary cleaning to get the surface clutter out of the way so she can get down to the nitty-gritty. That's what we tell ourselves anyway. In reality we just don't want her to know what slobs we are.

She does a great job, really great. This is a person who is personally offended by dirt, dust, and mildew. It's not a job, it's a crusade. She doesn't simply clean house, she eradicates dirt. She's good alright, but there's a catch. She is a compulsive talker, and when I say this I am not exaggerating.

"Gabby" (not her real name) is what I would classify as a "chain talker," meaning that she has the ability to flow seamlessly from one topic to the next without the need for any logically unifying thread, and can continue in this fashion for upwards of twenty minutes without ever seeming to draw a breath. Furthermore, she is unencumbered by that special need which hinders the average talker; namely, the requirement for another person to be listening. Often she does not even need another person to be on the premises. She loves to talk about house cleaning but is equally at ease suggesting the best stretches for lower back pain, a recipe for lime chutney, or why the toenail clippers they sell at Kant Spel drugstore (actual name: Rite Aid... really) are an inferior design.

But the clincher is that she is unable to conclude any conversation. Because everything reminds her of something else, she has no linear sense of a conversation's beginning and end. To call her thought process stream of consciousness doesn't do it justice, since streams are generally limited to flowing one direction at a time. "Flood" would be more like it. Any efforts to bring closure only produce the sensation that one is sinking in quicksand: the harder you struggle the more you get pulled back down.

After experiencing spectacular failures with cheap conversational devices such as "Wow, look at the time," and "I think I left the baby in the car with the motor running," I progressed to the bluntly elegant "I'm leaving" which yielded only slight improvement. In the end, nothing works gracefully, and one must turn and walk out the door, taking deep breaths as her words fade out behind you: "That reminds me, I was talking to this guy in the market and he said that his nephew…"

Nowadays I have to make plans to be out of the house when Gabby works. I put up with it because she does a great job cleaning. Besides, I hope to steer her toward the help she needs to overcome her challenge. I've told her about this new 12-step program for compulsive talkers… it's called On and On Anon.

TRAVELS WITH BABY: DOES BUNDLE OF JOY COUNT AS CARRY-ON BAGGAGE?

If airline travel makes you a little uneasy, try it with an infant. Under childless conditions, the incompetence, disorganization, and just plain tackiness of the airlines are good for a derisive chuckle, which can help distract your attention from that little voice in your brain saying "We're gonna crash We're gonna crash We're gonna crash..." Having a baby causes your body to produce abnormal amounts of Protective Hormone, which can severely impair your sense of humor to the point that you fail to see the fun in being trapped at 30,000 feet in a giant metal can with a belly full of flammable liquid and the aerodynamic properties of Raymond Burr.

It's bad enough that the check-in desks all look like used sets from old game shows and the security checkpoint is a diorama of minimum wage apathy. Once aboard the plane it is necessary to remind yourself that the flight attendant's safety presentation is not necessarily an indication of overall competence.

The way they stumble through it, you'd think they didn't give this speech several times a day. You can only hope that they devote a more serious effort to their other job duties, like handing out peanuts or serving as flotation devices in the event of a "water landing." They stammer and giggle, as though the other crew members have played a practical joke and handed them a copy of the text scrawled on the back of a cocktail napkin.

This time-honored skit is performed over a public address system that sounds like soup-can-and-string technology. When the pilot eventually comes on to mutter self-importantly about cruising altitudes and winds out of the southwest there's so much static, crackle, and hiss it makes him sound like he's broadcasting from Mars. How are they supposed to communicate to the tower when the back half of the plane seems to be out of range?

We sat in the tail section of the plane, so we were the last to get served our Sodium-Roasted Peanuts in a kevlar-graphite-mylar packet which can only be opened using both hands and your teeth. The packaging costs more than the nuts and can withstand fifty pounds of tensile pressure, at which point it tears open suddenly and scatters the nuts around the cabin. But if you gather up the pieces and actually eat them, they do their job, which is to make you thirsty and frustrated enough to buy a miniature four-dollar Bloody Mary.

Most airlines will permit you to take your baby along without purchase of an additional seat, provided you are able to hold the baby on your lap for the entire flight. Makes sense, right? Everyone says flying is safer than driving but with baby Emma relaxing on Julia's lap, it suddenly felt risky, just having her in our arms.

You can't do that in a car; they tell you scary stories about how hitting a pebble will catapult your baby into the next block. It started me thinking that a hefty chunk of turbulence would launch her headfirst into the ceiling pretty easily. Then I started feeling guilty for being too cheap to buy the additional seat.

I'm surprised the airline even gives you the choice, considering how strict they are about everything else. Too much slack in your seat belt gets you a rap on the knuckles (except in first class, where they tighten it for you and apologize for the inconvenience), and failure to stow carry-on luggage in the overhead bins or under the seat in front of you is now an act of high treason. In the event of turbulence they don't want briefcases, backpacks, and fruit baskets bouncing around the cabin whacking people, but show 'em an untethered 25-pound baby and all they do is start making goo goo talk.

Today's Travel Tip: If you have too much carry-on luggage, just disguise your extra bag as a big baby. You can board first and then hold it on your lap and periodically burp it. Believe me, no one will bother you. They won't even sit near you.

THE OLD BAWL GAME

Isolation can really sneak up on you. You may not notice that you've begun to refer to automobile accidents as "owies," or that you have begun to leave phone messages in sing-song Dr. Seuss rhyme schemes, and even your friends may be reluctant to point out these warning signs to you. In any case, should you ever find yourself drinking vodka from a Winnie The Pooh sippy-cup, it is time to strongly consider a little change of scenery.

My craving for social contact with Bigger People has escalated to the point that I am once again moonlighting as a Little League® baseball umpire. It is a great gig for anyone with a pure love of baseball who also doesn't mind wearing a uniform and telling others what to do. It is an exhilarating feeling, after all these months of infant care, to be around people with the intellectual sophistication and self-control of twelve-year-olds. Of course, I am referring to the coaches and league officials. The kids are great, too.

The Standard Infant Rules of Engagement shift from moment to moment, and are deeply rooted in the concept of "Right Now." You can't haul out a rule book and make an appeal for Nap Time. It is strictly the baby's call. So you can understand the satisfaction in officiating a game which is run by a very strict set of rules. Never mind that the Little League® rule book is so confusing that it seems to have been written in a country where baseball is not played and then translated back to English by someone with a bad sense of humor.

Being an umpire does present us with some scheduling conflicts. The early weeknight game starts at 5 PM which means I have to be there at 4:30 in order to break up the fist fight between the opposing coaches over which team gets to take infield practice first. Julia usually can't leave work till 5:00 so there is a window of an hour or so where we need to plan for baby care. This week I enlisted the help of my friend, Mark, whom Emma knows, and who figured an hour at the ballpark might make a nice little work break.

Ah, but nothing ever goes according to plan. Emma was not interested in eating in the afternoon before game time, and in my rush to get out the door I neglected to bring along a jar of baby food. No problem, I thought, Julia will be here soon enough. My greater concern at the time was to maintain my gruff authoritarian umpire's countenance as I approached the diamond pushing Emma in her stroller.

A small group of kids watched in confused silence as I pulled spare diapers, chew toys, and a supply of baby books from my duffel bag to outfit Mark for his short stint. Most of the moms thought it was pretty cute but I could tell the players were concerned. I could hear the muttering in the visitors dugout: Why does the Ump have a copy of *Pat The Bunny* sticking out of his pocket? I stayed with Emma as long as possible, talking goo-goo talk and making faces for her till it was time to run onto the field and bark out "Play ball!"

I can't remember what happened during the game because somewhere in the top of the first inning, Emma caught a whiff of the snack bar and decided that she was ready for that meal after all. Taking her cue from both coaches, she began to make her needs known at the top of her lungs.

Without a jar of baby food or a pair of lactating breasts, Mark was helpless. After the third out I sprinted to the bleachers to cuddle the baby and reassure Mark, but moments later I had to hand her back and dash back onto the field. And thus my routine was established.

Unfortunately, Julia was detained by a late-running meeting, and by the middle of the third inning my attention was badly divided. One coach began to question my powers of concentration, and his needling distracted me even more. The situation threatened to get out of control until I remembered my trusty little rule book. With a manner of authority I cited rule 9.01(b), which states, "Each umpire has authority to order a player or coach to do or refrain from doing anything which affects the administering of these rules..." On the basis of this rule I ordered him to go to the bleachers and help Mark read *Green Eggs And Ham* to Emma, so that I could get on with the business of running the game. When he protested on the grounds that nowhere does the rule book mention anything about hungry babies, I cited rule 9.01(c): "Each umpire has the authority to rule on any point not specifically covered in these rules." He didn't like it, but he agreed with the call. Rules are rules.

As luck would have it, Julia arrived and everything sorted itself out. Emma got her meal, the coach was allowed to skip the Dr. Seuss reading and return to his dugout, and I was able to direct my attention to the usual situations: runners on second and third with less than two outs, the runner on second leaves the base early as the batter, who turns out to be batting out of order, tries to hit an illegally-delivered pitch which hits the ground first but which also hits him at the same time as his swing is interfered with by the catchers glove. Ah, the simple pleasures.

CHILDCARE... THE C-WORD

I had planned on being a Homedaddy forever, until the other day when a careful study of our home videos confirmed my suspicion that Emma is growing. This is a shocker since I have not really been aware of time passing. In fact there have been several points, most notably, in the middle of the night when Emma is sick, when time has actually stood still. But there is no doubt about it, she is turning into a child, which is like a miniature person, only much louder.

At this rate, according to my calculations, she will eventually want to do crazy thing like have friends and go places with them. And where would I be then? A loopy house-husband with empty-nest syndrome, sitting in a tattered robe and my hair up in curlers, stuck in a catatonic rut of endless channel surfing.

In order to stave off this brutal fate I have realized that I must make certain preparations for easing myself back into the work force, which means that I will begin taking some sporadic freelance work. But where, I hear you asking, will Emma be when both Julia and I are working? It is a good question, and since neither of us have extended families in the area, we have begun to confront the C-word...

Childcare. It has such a brutal ring to it, after all these idyllic months of hanging around the house, changing diapers, doing dishes, and washing clothes... on the other hand maybe it doesn't sound so bad after all. But how am I going to find it? I'm a guy who agonizes over where to take my car for new brake pads.

I imagined the worst. I dreaded visiting the Lord Of The Flies Kiddy Kare Center, where adults take a hands-off approach to teaching societal boundaries, letting the older, more experienced children set a strong example for the younger ones. The curriculum encourages the children to develop valuable survival skills such as hunting wild pigs and building fires to signal for help.

If they didn't have an opening, we'd have to try Tater Tots (slogan: *For your little Couch Potato*), where all the kids are propped up in front of the tube in a filthy playroom where there are real potatoes growing in the sofa. The only soap on the premises for years has been the daily TV fare.

If we were still out of luck we'd have to move on to the All You Can Be Bootie Camp where discipline and duty are drilled into the little ones till they function like well-oiled machines. The program features finger painting, nursery rhymes, and of course, advanced weapons training.

In the end, as usual, the reality didn't come close to my paranoid fantasies. We found a wonderful daycare right in our neighborhood, run by a woman named Heidi who is so wonderfully sweet with the kids it would be nauseating if it weren't so totally genuine. We have begun taking Emma there for a few hours here and there, and the capper is that she really likes it.

True, she cries when we hand her over, but Heidi assured us that she cheers up as soon as we leave. I didn't take her word for it, though. I peeked through the window after stepping out the front door, and sure enough, as soon as she was sure I was out of earshot, it was party time. Made me wonder if it's a premonition of things to come.

IT WAS A VERY GOOD YEAR

The other day, as I watched Emma practice free-standing in the middle of the kitchen floor while maintaining a running commentary in her obscure dialect of Old Middle Infant, I was momentarily shaken by a vision of her no longer as a baby, but as an actual little kid. Given the efforts I've made adjusting to life with an infant (voted Most Improved by the Baby Association, Western Division), it's only understandable that I'd want to rest on my laurels for a while, or at least on my haunches. But no. Each new developmental milestone shakes the foundation of my carefully constructed little house of cards.

So, I've done the rational, responsible, adult thing and bought a new book about baby care... and none of these sissy newborn books either, this one is real serious stuff, evidenced by the hard-hitting, no-nonsense title, *Your One-Year-Old*. Lest the potential buyer remain unconvinced, the book is subtitled "12 to 24 months;" a shrewd marketing move which should satisfy the most exacting parent. I felt better even before I read it. The very act of seeking it out earned me the approval of the bookshop clerk, whose stony silence clearly spoke volumes. Plus, the time-honored technique of throwing money at a problem began to work its magic before I could even get the credit card back into my wallet.

I should have quit while I was ahead because the book itself was a big letdown. Here's an example of the top-secret parenting knowledge available to the reader only as a result of years of laboratory trials: "Your boy or girl is officially a One-year-old until the time of that second birthday, when he or she officially becomes a Two-year-old." Sounds like it was ghost written by Dan Quayle. All I learned was where to put the hyphens in the phrase "One-year-old." Not exactly earth-shattering, national security stuff.

I put the book to appropriate use propping up the short table leg and pondered Emma's and my situation. I have to buy new clothes, which are appropriate to her newly developing manual dexterity (still in the test stages) and her tactile interest in food. Used to be, a little puke on the shoulder was all I had to worry about. These days, anything smaller than a bread box gets softened up in her mouth and rubbed all over my shirt while I carry her. We give her these teething crackers which are like shortbread cookies which have been allowed to petrify under millions of pounds of pressure at the earth's core. They look like cookies, they smell like cookies, they chew like slate roofing tiles. But hey, what do babies know? We give it to her and say Have a cookie. We might as well hand her a maraca and say, Here, try a chicken leg, and remember to chew fifty times before you swallow.

She remains undaunted. Only baby saliva contains the secret ingredient necessary to soften the Mystery Teething Biscuit into a brown glue stick, which Emma rubs into my shirt, leaving a nasty little skid mark. This is a permanent skid mark, impervious to laundry soap, which lacks the solvent properties of baby spit. So, shirts must be wildly patterned, multi-colored, and easily washable. Preferably rubber so I can just hose off in the driveway.

In between loads of laundry, when I notice how fast Emma is growing up I get a stab of melancholy laced with panic. It isn't so much the feeling that I've squandered the fleeting magic of her infancy as much as the fact that I haven't yet exhausted my arsenal of infant jokes. I still try to crack wise about midnight feedings, cradle cap, and meconium (don't ask, don't tell) but there's a hollow ring to it. Must be the first pangs of Empty Jest Syndrome.

HOMEDADDY'S GUIDE TO MOTHER'S DAY

Mothers Day is the true test of the Homedaddy's mettle, the day when you must step back into the shadows, self-confident in your own abilities and achievements, while the spotlight shines on another. And while you're sulking and muttering in the shadows, don't forget to procure a modest (elaborate, by male standards) selection of gifts and flowers.

Flowers are absolutely essential to a successful Mother's Day. Most men are stumped at this level since they don't know the first thing about flowers, but you must not let this minor detail stop you. Like so many other personal choices and moral dilemmas you may face in life, the answer here is to take the high road and throw some money at the problem. Let's say you don't know a gladiolus from the American Gladiators. All you need to do is get on down to the florist, plunk down a wad of cash big enough to clog a wood chipper, and ask them to suggest a nice Mother's Day arrangement. They will not let you down. Not only will the bouquet be beautiful, but your mate will also know that they were not cheap. Don't ask me how this works; it just does. Expensive flowers say "You're the Greatest," while cheap flowers say "Well, you get the basic idea."

Another key element is food. Any successful orchestration of Mother's Day festivities requires a huge brunch with copious amounts of mimosas, a drink whose name derives from a Polynesian word meaning "let's get loaded before noon." The skilled Homedaddy must be expert at making one of two things: omelets or reservations. Bear in mind that Mother's Day is traditionally the busiest brunch day of the year, so you will need to make reservations a couple of years in advance unless you're going to Denny's for the Grand Slam® breakfast, in which case you might as well go with the cheap flowers.

It is always better to prepare the brunch at home, but if you do cook it yourself, it is a good idea to have at least one of your child's grandparents visiting so that they can play with Junior while you rattle the pots and pans and the honoree sleeps in.

You must also dress the baby up in some really special outfit in order to play this festivity thing to the hilt. Choose one of the very fancy party suits you received as a gift but which your baby never wears because they are so impractical for normal baby activities like throwing oatmeal. I selected a dainty pink frilly number, which was sent six months ago by some well-meaning friend with terrible taste. Emma, who is mostly a jeans-and-sweatshirt kind of gal, was already suspicious of this thing while it was still on its hanger. Dressing a baby under normal conditions is enough of a challenge, but when the child displays an active distrust for the garment, you have a situation on your hands.

I sang her one of her favorite songs, which didn't calm her down, but at least drowned out some of her protests. The biggest problem was the tiny neck-hole for the undershirt which was apparently supposed to be yanked down over a noggin the size of a crenshaw melon... what kind of morons design these things? It was like trying to stuff a bowling ball through a garden hose, but louder.

Eventually we reverted to the jeans-and-sweatshirt look. After all, wasn't the whole point of staying at home to Be Casual? And I'll be darned if Emma didn't look as cute as all get-out in her everyday duds. And with a brief crying fit under her belt, she was all smiles in time for the guest of honor. And the look on Emma's face when Julia walked into the room reminded me that I might be the one-and-only Homedaddy, but there's still no substitute for Mommy.

ZEN AND THE ART OF TEETHING

When things run smoothly with home and child, it is all too common for the Homedaddy to succumb to a momentary sense of adequacy. If allowed to flourish unchecked, this self-congratulatory state can blossom into a full-blown delusion of control. At this point there is bound to be some new development which brings reality back into sharper focus. If there is no such troubling new development, an old one can always re-surface.

Since Emma and I have been enjoying smooth sailing for a few days now, it was only to be expected that she resume teething. It's been a few months since she cut any teeth and I've grown more accustomed to admiring her little choppers than visualizing sharp bone slowly pushing through sensitive tissue. Forget the Tooth Fairy; this is the universe at work in all its random and violent glory.

A few months ago we co-starred in the first big disaster movie of infancy, "Teething: Gums of Agony." Now, at around 14 months of age, we find ourselves contractually obligated to star in the sequel, "Teething 2: Molar Hell."

This time it's worse. The molars push through more slowly than the front teeth, a fact she can appreciate more than ever with her rapidly developing awareness. Not like the old days when a little distraction went a long way. No more diverting her attention with a frozen dishrag to chew on or a few minutes of C-SPAN on the tube.

A quick web search on the word "teething" yielded the usual copiously redundant information as well as some new tidbits. One source claims that "...you may find that your baby gets relief if you rub the affected gum with your clean finger..." It's possible, but you may also find that Baby does not wish to have your finger rubbing on the Most Painful Spot in the World. If you don't already know how hard she can bite, you soon will. Keep the phone nearby to call 911 for the Jaws of Life to extricate your finger.

Another article suggested giving Baby a plastic chew toy, especially one that can be chilled or frozen. This seemed like a good idea till I read the next article which claimed that "...certain baby rattle and teething toys contain a softening chemical that causes cancer in laboratory animals..." Oh, great. I checked it out with The Consumer Product Safety Commission but their statement didn't provide much reassurance: "...parents of young children who mouth these products for long periods of time may wish to dispose of them," and I assume they mean the chew toy.

The rest of the web sites suggest pain-relief medication, which is OK, provided you can actually get the medicine into the baby. In the throes of teething, babies will often mistake the medicine dropper for a branding iron, and will exhibit the appropriate level of resistance. The bottle should come with a warning: "Attempts to stick a medicine dropper into the mouth of a thrashing baby with throbbing gums can result in more trouble than you want to know about."

Administering unwanted medicine to a baby is like giving a pill to a cat except that it is still socially permissible to grab a cat by the scruff of the neck and tilt the head back before prying the jaws open. Even then, the cat forgets the whole business a minute later while a one-year-old will glare at you for days as if memorizing the face of pure evil.

It is true, however, that there exists a perfect Zen state when you become one with your baby and can administer the dropper-full of medicine, thus allowing the healing energies to flow from the original packaging into the baby. I only wish I could tell you how to achieve that state.

Sometimes the best solution is just to keep your baby company and maintain a soothing demeanor. And instead of painkillers, stick to the Zen approach, and that way, perhaps you and the baby can, um, transcend dental medication.

AN IN-TENTS WEEKEND

New carpeting really stinks, as in, smells bad. Looks great, absolutely fabulous, but smells like a solvent factory. It isn't enough to say that the old carpeting was bad. It was so dirty it was colorless; it was so dense with grime that it trapped light in its gravitational field, leaving rooms hopelessly dim despite the high-wattage bulbs.

Visually, the new carpet solved this problem, but it caused an air quality issue in our home due to a phenomenon called "off-gassing," a phrase which is pretty self-explanatory. So we decided to go camping for the weekend and get some fresh air.

I love to go camping but I am still not much of a camper. I have been on many trips, but always with other people who know what they're doing. I do know that there must be a campfire and it is my duty to poke at it with a stick, attempting to rearrange the logs just perfectly, never giving up until the fire is stone dead. The closest I ever came to camping as a kid was watching Fess Parker as the TV Daniel Boone. Roughing it meant eating over the sink while I watched the show.

Packing for camping with a baby is pretty easy, since you have become used to packing a survival kit every day. You can hardly walk to the corner for a newspaper without a backpack full of diapers, wipes, plastic pants, a plastic bag for trash, extra clothes, a handful of small toys, a sippy-cup, a few jars of food, a baggy of little snacks, a first aid kit, a week's supply of water, a cell phone.

Actually getting on the road is the hard part. It is necessary to make many last-minute dashes back into the house after you've actually reached the driveway and have the car doors open. Leaving the house with a baby is a time warp, and so is leaving to go camping. Their combined effect can send you spinning in a crazy figure-eight orbit with your front door being the center point. You shoot out the front door, thinking you are leaving to go camping, but you realize that you've forgotten to start the dishwasher, so your energy shifts and you arc over the top of the orbit and go whizzing back through the front door. While starting the dishwasher you realize you've forgotten the Scrabble game, so you grab it as you once again get sucked out the front door. This time your momentum carries you all the way out to the

BZZZZzzzzzzz

car, where something jogs your memory and sends you flying back into the house for the maple syrup for Saturday morning's pancakes.

A sufficiently absent-minded person can remain in such an orbit for hours. Each time you complete an orbit and shoot through the front door you can only hope to have gained sufficient escape velocity to break free of your home's gravitational field. Do not try to estimate your actual time of departure without an Astronomy Ph.D.

The great thing about camping is that you learn something every time. This time I learned that mosquitoes really like babies.

We arrived at our campsite in the late afternoon and the word must have been out on the mosquito grapevine because they were waiting for us.

As soon as we stepped out of the car, they rallied around the fresh meat. Emma, in particular, was considered a delicacy. A cloud of them seized her and began to carry her off but we grabbed hold of a dangling foot and pulled her back.

But what do you do for repellent? You can't just douse them with the same stuff they use to fumigate houses. Most bug repellents have warnings about poisoning small children. We just whisked her into the tent, pronto, and waited for them to thin out after the sun went down.

They say that garlic is a good bug repellent, and that if you eat enough of it the bugs won't bother you, and in fact, neither will other people. Must have something to do with off-gassing. Since it is a questionable practice to feed a baby enough garlic to repel bugs, I suggest you eat the garlic and just keep that baby hugged close against you as much as possible. You'll both feel so good you won't care about a few mosquito bites, and the garlic aroma will probably overpower the new carpet smell after you return home.

A GAME OF CAT AND MOUSE

Real live animals hold a special fascination for babies and small children, a fascination we encourage by providing stuffed toy versions for their amusement and comfort. But even the favorite stuffed-critter doll pales by comparison to the real thing. Emma has always loved her kitty-cat dolls, but she is absolutely infatuated with our cat, 99.

99, named after Secret Agent 99 from "Get Smart," is not what you would call a lovey-dovey cat. She does not wish to be picked up or held in laps, and these wishes are communicated via the international language of pain. She isn't exactly ornery so much as standoffish. She is understated. I know that deep down, she regards me with a special love and devotion, which she regularly expresses by allowing me to put food into her dish.

Some cats are good with children, which means that they will absorb hours of torture before hauling their paunch off the sofa and reeling out to the yard for a nap in the sun. Our friend's cat, Astro, a Persian Boneless, is such a specimen; you have to use both arms when picking him up to keep him from pouring onto the ground. 99 is no such creature. Pick her up and she uses your chest as a launching pad. As we used to say in the 90's, she places a high value on her personal space.

Naturally, Emma's enthusiasm to play with the kitty is a cause of concern in this house. Baby-to-cat contact must be limited to a few closely supervised sessions. We used to think that Emma would be safe as long as 99 had an escape route, but all it took was one good handful of kitty ear to blow a big hole in that theory. I saw the whole thing. 99 struck like lightning with a quick chop to the forehead, then suddenly vanished with a puff of smoke and a bullet-riccochet sound effect. I had already swept Emma up into my arms and was cooing to her by the time the pain registered in the forehead area. Judging from her continued interest in the cat, I'd say she still has no idea what happened.

Besides being an emergency room visit waiting to happen, 99 presents another dilemma. Her practice of ritual mouse killing is exposing Emma to certain grim food chain realities not otherwise covered in the standard infant literature. 99 does not simply kill a mouse; she parades before us while chewing on the struggling wretch and singing a warbling kitty-victory song until we acknowledge her, and it is only then that she gets down to business.

This is probably not news to you cat owners, but mice are apparently very crunchy; if you didn't know better, you might think the cat was eating a bag of potato chips. There is nothing about this in *Sylvester the Musical Mouse,* or in the Beatrix Potter Nursery Rhymes. Even the graphic rodent mutilations of *Three Blind Mice* cannot compare to the spectacle of 99 crushing a mouse's skull in her jaws while we egg her on and Walt Disney turns over in his grave, or his frost-free Amana, or wherever he is.

Of course we encourage her. Mouse eradication is one of the great benefits of cat ownership. Stuffed toys are great but real mice are pests. Mickey Mouse isn't exactly known for tunneling into your kitchen, eating your cereal, and leaving little cartoon mouse droppings in the cupboards.

The downside is that Emma, at one year of age, is already being exposed to life's inconsistencies, which during the teenage years become known as hypocrisy. The upside is that she has learned the zoologically accurate lyric to the verse in *Old MacDonald* wherein "On that farm he had a mouse, E-I-E-I-O:

"With a crunch crunch here and a crunch crunch there,
Here a crunch, there a crunch, everywhere a crunch crunch..."

Meanwhile, her loyal old stuffed Mousie doll sits in the corner saying nothing. Maybe the cat got his tongue.

CURIOUS GEORGE REVISITED

There are two types of readers. First is the discriminating reader, devoted entirely to "quality" books and articles. Next comes the group to which I belong, comprised of folks who merely require visual distraction. A classic work, biography, or current satire is always preferable, but a piece of junk mail or the back of a cereal box will do just fine.

Since the appearance of baby Emma, however, my reading list has taken a new slant, which owes everything to the sudden and merciless invasion of children's books into our home. A notable entry in this category, and today's subject, is *Curious George Visits an Amusement Park*.

Those of you exposed to children's literature are no doubt familiar with the Curious George series, in which a mysterious operative known cryptically as "the man with the yellow hat" systematically leads George the monkey through an urban litany of insults and injuries. In each installment, the man leaves George alone in a situation where a monkey would otherwise require total supervision, with the result that George is both socially and technologically out of his league. Predictably, all you-know-what breaks loose, and only the sudden and inexplicably coincidental reappearance of the man with the yellow hat can restore order.

The reader is never made privy to any useful information about the man with the yellow hat. What is his work, where is his family, and why does he live alone with a monkey?

In the opening panel of this book, the man with the yellow hat's suggestion to visit an amusement park instantly makes the reader uneasy, and why not? The whole setup smacks of disaster. Why take a monkey to an amusement park? George is excited by the idea, but this in itself is not significant. He worships the man with the yellow hat and would be just as happy had the man's notion been to spend the afternoon trimming his nose hairs. The plot gets jump-started just two panels later, when he leaves George alone in front of the ticket booth with a handful of cash.

At the risk of spoiling the ending, I'll let it slip that George commits breaking and entering, larceny, and resisting arrest in short order. But in a really cute way. Of course, he thinks he is doing the right thing... what the heck was it that the man with the yellow hat wanted him to do? Then, via a blatantly contrived plot device, George evades his would-be captors long enough to stop and watch the roller coaster at the very moment that his friends, Yvonne and her Aunt Ruby hurtle past with such force that Aunt Ruby loses her purse, enabling George to prove his worth by climbing the roller coaster to retrieve her valuables just as the ticket seller and his gang of angry thugs catch up with him.

If Martin Scorcese ever directs the film version, this is the point in the story where George would get cornered in the parking lot and beaten with baseball bats and fireplace pokers for about ten minutes before being stuffed into a gunney sack and tossed into the trunk of a car.

Yep, things look mighty bad indeed for George until, as usual, the man with the yellow hat shows up on cue and all threats evaporate. The reader can only imagine him pushing crisp Franklins into the hands of the amusement park security guards just beyond the borders of the illustrations.

The underlying message seems to be that the natural curiosity of children leads first to low comedy, then danger, and finally, redemption at the hands of authority. It is a brilliant cautionary tale warning of the dangers of codependency. When someone expects too much of you, don't try to meet their expectations. And remember: ignorance is no defense. Every time I read it to Emma I wonder if she is soaking it all up.

George never gets punished, since a guy spanking his monkey in a children's book would incur the wrath of animal rights activists and censors alike.

Maybe it really is just a simple tale of a guy and his monkey.

APPROVAL RATINGS DROP DURING HOMEDADDY'S WEEK OFF

My wife, Julia, went off to a conference in another state and took Emma with her. They'll be gone for five more days, and I hardly know what to do with myself. In the few short days they've been gone I can already feel my technique starting to get rusty.

Naturally, I think I've been doing very well so far, but we are not always the best judges of ourselves. I certainly never expected the jolt I received this morning when I picked up my copy of *Father Times,* a Homedaddy trade journal, and read the cover story:

APPROVAL RATINGS

Homedaddy's Confidence Tumbles Today, Report Cites Worries About Short-Term Outlook.

   Homedaddy's confidence rating sagged seven points today and now stands at an all-time low. It was the largest daily decline since the 7.9-point drop recorded the last time he took Emma to the pediatrician for immunizations. Along with concerns about the short-term laundry outlook, his lack of presence is a primary reason for today's decline. The Diaper Index, which has a strong track record in predicting future activity, fell nearly 11 points to close at 95.9 last month. The Teething Situation Index decreased only one and a half points and now stands at 171.2.

   According to the Male Parent Research Center, "Tumultuous teething developments, airline travel, and unsettling nap patterns have been major factors in curbing Homedaddy's popularity, and his notable absence this week isn't helping. Although

Homedaddy continues to be generally confident about current baby conditions, he will have to be in peak form upon the return home of wife and child. Homedaddy has traditionally tended to rebound rapidly from sporadic downturns in the infant and toddler sectors."

Industry-wide, some 48% of dads surveyed say current conditions are "good," while 32% say naps are "sufficient" up from a little less than 29% in the fourth quarter.

It was a wake-up call. An off-season training regimen was called for. I tried to work on my mechanics by carrying a more or less life-sized doll around the house, but it lacked the heft and will power to make a worthwhile exercise. When this didn't work I studied the videotapes. The home video camera is a fabulous tool for deconstructing the physical techniques of childcare. While my performance was consistent, the replays made it clear that my diaper changing stance is too wide. I could also see that I am not keeping my wrist straight when spoon-feeding. Definitely room for improvement.

I simply must bring these rating points up and I can't do it while sitting on the bench. When Emma returns I am going to have my team of pollsters define the substantial issues, and then I am going to address them proactively. Even if it means reading Curious George yet again.

FATHER'S DAY RAIN CHECK

My first Father's Day didn't really count; Emma was three months old, and at that time you could have told me I had won the lottery and it probably wouldn't have penetrated my bliss-riddled skull. I was hardly sleeping at all, as much from excitement as from Emma waking up, with the result that things had never seemed so silly to me since I was a freshman in college and we went to that party with the really funny-tasting punch.

Twelve months later, with the concept of fatherhood finally beginning to establish a foothold in my brain, I was alone on Father's Day. Julia and Emma were out of the state, combining business with pleasure by attending a conference and visiting with family.

Even though I was all alone, knocking around the house on Father's Day, I didn't feel left out. The date itself doesn't hold much meaning for me, since I come from a family where these kinds of specifics are not very important. It isn't that I can't remember birthdays and other important dates, it's just that I have trouble connecting this knowledge with the fact of physical existence on that particular day, which creates conversations like this:

Julia: Isn't it your father's birthday today?

Me: No.

Julia: Isn't his birthday the twelfth?

Me: Yes.

Julia: Well, today is the twelfth.

Me: OK fine, if you're gonna nitpick...

Predictably, I've become a master of the belated birthday gift. Sometimes they are so late I just pretend they're early for the next year, which sets the dangerous precedent of appearing to be on top of these things.

When I told a friend of mine I was alone, he claimed that the only purpose of Fathers Day is to allow your family to relieve their guilt for the way they treat you the rest of the year, and so it was just as well they were out of town. He figured I could save it up for a rainy day.

I did a load of laundry, and since I was temporarily a swingin' bachelor again, I got a little wild and mixed my whites and my colors. In between cycles, I watched a baseball game on the tube. When Julia called to wish me a happy Father's Day I probably sounded wistful and distant, when in fact I was scrutinizing an instant replay... the second-base umpire had definitely blown the call on the double-play pivot...

It didn't occur to me until later that it might have made her feel rotten, so I was unprepared for the windfall of attention and affection upon their return. Turned out we celebrated a belated Father's Day this weekend. They took me out to see the Giants-Dodgers game.

...CURVEBALL, GOT 'EM LOOKING!

TELL IT LIKE IT SEEMS

As babies grow into toddlerhood and begin to speak, there is a phase where they repeat everything you say. This poses a tremendous challenge to those parents who use expletives the way others breathe oxygen. You may break this habit, but the urge never goes away. Calling someone a "doo doo head" will never carry the visceral impact of comparing them to an orifice usually covered by at least two layers of clothing.

Despite your best efforts, you'll blurt it out now and then, and your child will repeat it mechanically long before she knows what it means. Once she learns what it means she will repeat it even more often. You must adopt what is known in football as the "prevent defense." Besides disarming your arsenal of curses, you'll also have to invent cutesy secret code phrases for sex (if you ever run into me at a party, ask me about the laundry joke).

This is the beginning of the long and painful process of deciding how much to lie to your children. Don't tell me you never lie to your children, or to anyone for that matter. Everyone lies, at least by omission, which, according to my elementary school principal, amounted to the same thing.

Lying, hiding the truth, putting your best spin on a situation, or writing advertising, it's all the same, and I am not saying that's always a bad thing. Very young children are not equipped to comprehend the horrors of war crimes, industrial waste, and the Iowa Caucuses.

Lies must be understood as an ingrained part of our culture. Consider, for example, the ad campaign for a popular soft drink which I would never be so tacky as to name (Sprite) which claims that "Image Is Nothing." Yeah sure. This is why they have an annual television advertising budget that could eliminate world hunger and possibly even cure my former boss of standing too close and spitting when he talks.

So what do you do? Last weekend we went to the Ballpark Formerly Known As Candlestick to see the Giants and the Dodgers. I figured we'd get tickets at the park, day of the game, from some helpful soul I meet standing around near the main box office.

I don't buy tickets from "scalpers;" that would be illegal. I just find someone who wishes to give me the tickets as a gift, which is not so

difficult as you might imagine. The world is full of generous people. We met a guy who was happy to give us some excellent tickets simply because we asked for them. It was a wonderful display of spontaneous generosity for Emma to witness.

Naturally, I wanted to teach her that when someone does something nice for you, it is important to be nice in return so I lent the guy some money which, we figured, he can pay back when the Cubs win the Series (by which time the interest alone will be more than the national debt).

Lies, spin, omission, double standards... call it what you will. Here at Homedaddy® Corporate Headquarters we refer to it as Selective Positive Imaging. Equally effective when spread around on flower beds. Send for a free brochure.

NOTES FROM THE SLEEP-DEPRIVED

The greatest gift you can give your children is to stay awake through most of their childhood, although this is turning out to be easier said than done. It never used to be an issue, back in the days of Newborn Euphoria, back before I learned the awful truth: Babies are easy... children are hard.

When Emma was first born I felt as though the rest of my life had been a dream, and I was now living in a more vivid reality. Little did I realize that this process would not stop. These days, I feel so hyper-aware that it makes Emma's infancy seem like an old grainy newsreel.

With each day, everything becomes so much more focused that it doesn't seem possible. I wake up thinking "Please, no more, no closer, I am aware of plenty, I can make out the detail just fine," but no; it's as though the big focus ring on the lens of the universe gets nudged again and some additional unnecessary but compelling details pop into view.

I can remember feeling like there was a lot going on; like I had no time to get anything done. Ha ha ha, that was back in the days of yore when Emma took two naps a day. Two naps! What a luxury! Why, the things I could do with an extra hour in the morning! I could earn a real estate license, or a home-study graduate degree. I could rake the leaves and fix the fence, I could become an artist. I'd take a class in Figure Drawing, learn how to draw some figures. I'd say six figures ought to do it.

On second thought, I'd probably just take a nap. Maybe this over-aware state which a friend of mine calls "Tracking The World" is nothing more than a symptom of sleep deprivation. Yeah, that's it, that's the answer... more sleep!

In my dreams, I guess. In the meantime, the solution is coffee, although the stuff I brew at home is actually more of a paste than a solution. I am a coffee snob, and usually strive to grind fresh, organic beans and brew a little pot of espresso, a concentrated tincture of caffeine guaranteed to get my attention when it most needs getting. It's so thick that when I get tired of drinking it I just massage some into my temples.

Oddly enough, fancy coffee doesn't get me as jittery as the really cheap stuff, the kind that tastes like volcanic ash mixed with scalding brown water and is customarily served in Styrofoam cups. If you want to get wired, forget espresso; the Workingman's Blend will have you humming like a tuning fork after a cup and a half. I just need a boost, not the night terrors, so I stick to the quality beans.

Since the only time left in my day for writing is usually between the hours of 4 and 6 AM, it feels only natural to be writing about coffee. I might feel differently when it starts to wear off later on, right around the time when Emma used to take her morning nap.

STAY COOL

At some point after the first year, babies turn into toddlers and make the transition from being totally dependent and insatiable to being verbal and mobile as well. Most experts agree that a sense of order and routine is important to help the young one feel familiar in the home environment.

Of course, when you travel, all of that stuff goes out the window. The practical realities of traveling are often at odds with a baby's desires. Babies do not want to get to the airport hours before departure time, but until they get organized and raise a substantial amount of lobbying money, they aren't going to see any concessions in this area.

Flying with really little babies is easy. As long as Mommy is on hand, there usually isn't much the father needs to do besides function as a Sherpa for the expedition, carrying huge loads of baby-support equipment into hostile environments such as hotel lobbies, truck stops, and relatives' homes.

Once babies get verbal and mobile, you've got another thing on your hands. Keeping a toddler confined to an airplane seat requires more than a backpack full of toys, books, dolls, food and water. You also need a measure of luck, and if your child is a climber, it is important to have a very understanding person in the seat in front of you.

During our last trip I made a major breakthrough when I

discovered, through a very scientific process, that Emma likes to eat ice. My method consisted of having her point at my glass and yell "Ice!" The cubes were too big for her, so I had to fish one out of the glass with my fingers, pop it into my mouth, bite it into pieces of a more reasonable size, spit them back into the palm of my hand and then offer them to her. She would consider the various pieces, nodding and saying "ice" until she made her selection.

This kept the two of us busy but seemed to distract the guy sitting next to me. I could tell he wasn't very fond of babies because every time I would spit out some newly-reduced cubes into the palm of my hand he would look over with a pained expression that said he hoped we wouldn't be keeping this up for long.

Some people claim that ice cubes of any size should be considered a choking hazard, but the very fact that it was ice felt like a built-in safety net to me. As long as it isn't a fist-sized chunk, she can't very well choke on it before it melts, right? Even so, in the event of An Episode I could always wrap a blanket around her neck to encourage a faster thaw. Maybe a blow drier aimed at the throat would work even better.

Happily, she didn't choke, and the ice cube routine kept her entertained while keeping her gums numb enough to ignore those molars slowly boring their way through. I was still nervous, though, since flying scares me when I start to think about it too hard, so I borrowed Emma's pacifier. Worked like a charm, although it was just about the last straw for the guy next to me. I shrugged it off as his problem, figuring I did the airline a favor since he bought four drinks during a two-hour flight. I wondered how he would have reacted if I'd asked the flight attendant to bring me a blow drier.

NINE LIVES OF A STUFFED CAT

Even though this isn't the obit page, I feel compelled to mention the passing of "Kitty", a small stuffed tabby cat, a gift to Emma from her friend Rich. Kitty enjoyed celebrity status as one of Emma's favorite stuffed companions, sharing the honors with "Darla," a floppy little tart in the Raggedy Ann vein who catapulted to stardom after being discovered in the bottom of a bargain bin at a South Dakota thrift shop.

According to the tag on her leg, Kitty's given name was Tabitha, a moniker as pretentious as it was cumbersome and inaccessible to the infant tongue. Show business legend has it that a four-month-old Emma, first laying eyes upon the Fabric Feline, as she came to be known in the trades, pointed and actually said "Kitty," or at any rate, a guttural one-syllable utterance, and the nickname stuck.

With a deadpan expression to rival the great Buster Keaton, Kitty brilliantly portrayed Emma's trusty sidekick in dozens of slapstick episodes in which she invariably endured the comically brutal trials and tribulations associated with being owned by a baby. She was squeezed, bitten, swung by the tail, dipped in creamed spinach, and fed to the dog.

On screen, her stony countenance never registered a flicker of emotion, but the demands and pressures left their mark. Her private life was said to be a shambles; there were hushed whispers about her excesses. Repeated visits to the washing machine to "get clean" were only more grist for the rumor mill.

Kitty's greatest role was co-starring opposite Emma as the Non-Seatbelted Stroller Passenger in the still-running serial *Emma and Papa Go To The Store,* an action series light on plot and heavy on cheap stroller stunts. In each episode, Emma waits till Daddy is not looking and then drops Kitty over the side of the stroller. Comic tension builds as the audience waits to see how far back towards home will they get before Homedaddy discovers Kitty is missing. Then, how far back will they have to walk to find her?

Sometimes she's sitting in the middle of the sidewalk ten feet back. Sometimes she lands in the middle of the crosswalk. She turns up in gutters, in the middle of parking lots, and in Kant Spel drugstore sitting astride the little cigarette shelf behind the cashier.

No such luck this time. We re-traced our steps all the way back to the store and through the aisles. We even asked the cashiers if anyone had seen her. No dice. We stumbled home in a daze, struggling to make sense of it all.

But wait a minute, is that... could it be... Kitty! With her head jammed through the spokes and her body wrapped around the stroller axle! I guess I shouldn't be surprised. With a show this popular, they'd never kill off one of the main characters. No wonder that stroller was getting so hard to push ...

UNDERSTANDING BABY'S FIRST WORD

Children develop at different rates, and parents just need to learn to relax, since your child will walk and talk when he is darn well ready. Some babies are ready to compete in the Iron Man Triathlon at nine months even though they might be communicating in grunts and crude hand gestures well into their early thirties, while other babies show no interest whatsoever in walking, and instead prefer to sit in the middle of the floor reciting the periodic table of elements.

The very notion of "baby's first word" is a popular myth, since most parents cheat by putting their face three inches away from the child, often frightening the tar out of him, while chanting "Say mama, mah-mah, SAY MAMA!" until the little one, in a desperate act of self-preservation, finally blurts out a badly garbled version. The proud parents then phone friends and relatives to spread the news and then send away for a Mensa application. Never mind that the baby doesn't know the true meaning and application of the word any more than he knows the melting point of tungsten.

This does not count as baby's first word. It is merely the first introduction to the art of "apple polishing," which is, of course, better known by another anatomically-based phrase which is so crude that I could not possibly publish it here and instead must rely on the probability that you know exactly what I am talking about and in fact are thinking of it at this very moment.

Many parents are full of stories (among other things) about how their child's first word was "ratio," or "jurisdiction, "and they will tell you these tales with such wide-eyed belief that you will either have to make an awkward excuse to leave or use your pepper spray.

According to a very scientific poll conducted by the Homedaddy® Research Institute, the first legitimate word of 99% of all babies is "no." It is actually a very complex word with many shades of meaning, depending on inflection, facial expression, body english, volume, and duration. A gently murmured "no" could mean "maybe," whereas a 30-second, high-volume, red-in-the-face number could actually mean "no."

Toddlers spend most of their time in a frustrated condition, since they lack the verbal skills to express their concerns. Questions as "Why does evil exist," "Do we really have free will," and the ever-popular "Is there a God" must all be posed using words like "ba-ba," "mama," and "joos," which makes a straight answer unlikely. Thus begins the age of tantrums, where Baby will vent his rage by rolling on the floor, kicking and screaming.

In college, your child will learn that this is called an "existential crisis," and will be able to deal with it in a more mature fashion. He'll go to parties where, inspired by dangerously loud music and forbidden refreshments, he will roll on the floor kicking and screaming with lots of other students pondering the same questions. A straight answer will be as elusive as ever.

CRAYONS HAPPEN

Wilson the Giant Black Labrador has always been a source of great amusement to Emma. She is thoroughly entertained by watching him eat dog food from his bowl, while feeding him by hand is even better. Funniest of all is to toss food for him to catch.

I have to admit, a hundred-plus pounds of wild-eyed, floppy-eared dog lunging around the kitchen for a single piece of kibble is pretty silly. Emma thinks it's a riot.

The very word "kibble" cracks her up, and it is indeed a word which is difficult to take seriously. She holds up a piece for scrutiny and asks, "Whuzzat?" I try to keep a straight face as I say, "kibble," but it's not easy. You try it sometime.

Dogs have their own logic, and I try to consider this as I wonder whether Wilson is a very picky eater, or just dumb as a bag of hammers. At times he will decline to touch the perfectly good food in his bowl, but if you pick up a single piece and feign throwing motions he goes all to pieces and starts knocking over bookcases with his tail. He'll catch and eat as many pieces of kibble as you care to throw.

For Emma, the thought of kibble being funny eventually yields to other trains of baby thought, leaving behind a generally positive feeling about this Thing Called Kibble. Since she's still holding a piece of it in her hand it is only a matter of time before she considers the possibility of eating it herself, and since all associations thus far are good ones, I have to intervene before she goes through with it.

Not to be an alarmist, but you really don't want your child eating dog food. Just think about the *World's Worst Cuts of Beef*; little specks of offal so remote and disgusting that they can't even rightfully be called cuts. Believe it or not, there is meat that exceeds even the USDA's allowable human consumption levels for bacteria, rat hairs, and insect larvae. Try to imagine meat too trashy even for the fast-food industry. This is what they use to make dog food.

Wilson will eat anything if you toss it to him, and Emma discovered that he'll even eat crayons if you pretend they are doggie treats. I knew I should discourage Emma from following up on this discovery, but I was laughing too hard..

But as the old saying goes, you reap what you sow. One of Homedaddy's many duties is to scoop up the dog poop in the yard on the day before each week's trash pickup, although I hesitate to use the word "poop" here. It's acceptable when talking about babies, but when applied in association with a dog of this size, it just trivializes things. I think a phrase like "Gross National Product" is more like it. In any case, it isn't possible to do this chore and remain ignorant of the fact that Wilson has eaten several dozen of Emma's crayons. I won't burden you with the details, except to say the results are very '60s.

Wilson always has been a very colorful character.

LAUNDRY BLUES

Some people still do not realize how boring laundry can be. I'm talking about real laundry, not the student version where you go once every six months with a hundred bucks in quarters, and you go in the middle of the night so you can run sixteen machines at once.

Housewives have known it for centuries; the new Homedaddies are just now figuring it out: Doing the laundry is a drag. Never mind the fact that it's an uphill battle you'll never win; the worst part is that it exposes you to dangerously unhealthy levels of boredom. If allowed to continue unchecked, this can lead to Laundry Shock Syndrome, a degenerative state of apathy toward the world at large which is not covered by your medical plan.

This unfortunate condition cannot be cured but it can be prevented, and you working mommies hold the key. By utilizing the Homedaddy Laundry Concept® you can turn this blindingly dull activity into a game of wits and wiles... a tantalizing brain teaser, a high fashion treasure hunt, and a test of nerves and manual dexterity all rolled into one! Here's how it works:

1. Never throw clothing of any kind into a hamper. Would you want your husband to be able to locate all of the dirty clothes in a room merely by picking up a hamper? Of course not. So get creative: Under the bed, under the car seats, and wedged behind the toilet are good places to start. Do not be hindered by conventional notions of civilized behavior.

2. By using the patented Homedaddy Clump Concept®, you can create mounds of clothing which contain customized blends of dirty clothes, mostly-clean clothes to be worn again, and silk and rayon items of great value which must be dry cleaned only. Nothing can compare to the sense of satisfaction at a job well done that a Homedaddy feels after sorting through a pile of clothes only to wind up with several new piles.

3. Always remove articles of clothing so they end up inside-out, and preferably so that they are wrapped up inside each other. Turn the laundry into a job for a man who works with his hands! Remember: Any wimp could just dump the hamper into the washer... but you need a real Homedaddy® to handle your load! What better way to let him know!

4. Your secret weapon: Pockets! By strategically leaving things in your pockets, you can elevate the Homedaddy Laundry Concept® to new heights. The industry standard for this technique is lipstick, preferably a shade with a name like "Heather Mist" or "Baked Raisin." This will guarantee that it creates stains of a different color than anything else in your wardrobe, or in the known physical universe for that matter. But don't limit yourself to lipstick. Cash, birth certificates, the house deed... the sky's the limit!

I won't lie to you. The Homedaddy Laundry Concept® requires a great deal of additional commitment on the part of you working mommies, who are already weakened from exposure to fluorescent light and bad coffee in Styrofoam cups. It is asking a lot of you to fight against your natural drive for cleanliness and order, but it is a sacrifice you will make if you want to let your Homedaddy know he's needed.

BABY MANICURE IS A NAIL-BITER

"I have found the best way to give advice to your children is to find out what they want and then advise them to do it." — Harry S. Truman

This statement is, of course, exactly the type of smarmy, self-important bull-product you would expect to hear from a man who never had to trim a baby's fingernails.

Fingernail trimming is not something routinely covered in childbirth or parenting classes. They're too busy telling you about the real exciting stuff like cradle cap and meconium (don't ask, don't tell).

In the first few days it's not that big a deal. Mom just bites them off, and since she is generally spending her waking hours kissing the baby all over, the Little Prototype never even notices. This is a good thing, since newborns tend to wave their arms and legs around in random swirling motions which make long fingernails a serious hazard.

A baby will be lying there, peaceful as a monk on Prozac, and then suddenly lash out with a combination of moves that looks like a new martial art. It would make a good Kung Fu movie: Babies of the Shao Lin Temple. Since they can't yet speak, you can amuse yourself by dubbing in the dialogue for them: "Ahh, you fight like a wetnurse... now you must die!"

In the early days, they are mostly dangerous to themselves since they haven't really learned where their bodies end and the outside world starts. All of that random waving and grabbing eventually results in self-contact, which is the usual explanation for babies with scratches on their faces.

A few months down the road, though, is another story, when the fingernails, left untrimmed, become actual talons, and the unsuspecting parent leaning in for that one last smooch gets a nasty surprise.

Mother Nature being the prankster that she is, a baby's new-found strength and agility after about four months will correspond to the fingernails getting a little tougher. If they are not closely trimmed, you run the risk of having a meatball-sized chunk of flesh torn from your cheek.

By this time you need to graduate to nail clippers. You can use the regular kind, although you can also buy special baby versions which feature pink and blue bunnies on the impossible-to-open bubble wrap packaging and are also, incidentally, totally useless.

Babies are, on the whole, suspicious of any grown-up murmuring sweet nothings while wielding a sharp metal object. You can expect resistance. The fact that you then end up having to pin them between your legs in a scissors-grip will only reinforce their apprehensions. The escalated struggle will then increase the odds that you will inflict some sort of cuticle-related injury.

Perhaps what is needed is a Baby Fingernail-Trimming Service. No one has done it yet... maybe this will be my claim to fame. I'll call it the Talon Agency.

ALL TODDLERS ARE HIPPIES

One of my greatest fears of parenthood was that I'd have to attend kiddy music sing-alongs. As it turned out, I didn't know what I'd been missing.

Every Wednesday night there is a kids' music concert in our local ice cream parlor. A very nice woman named Susan Kessey sets up a tiny little stage with her guitar and her microphone, as well as another microphone on a stand about two feet high, as though Billy Barty was going to make a guest appearance singing backup, but no such luck, of course, it is just an open mike for any child with dreams of glory.

Susan also provides several baskets of party supplies: drums, shakers, xylophones, tambourines, kazoos and other instruments; plus a pile of wild scarves and costume jewelry. You can say one thing, she knows her audience. These kids have come to party.

I was unprepared for the wave of pure hedonistic abandon that washed over us as we walked in the door. It was a scene to rival the best rock concerts I've ever attended, and that's saying something.

There was free-form dancing, group drumming, nakedness, costumes, scarves, painted faces, and even a couple of kids standing alone in a corner talking to themselves or to imaginary entities. And every last one of 'em stoned to the gills on ice cream. Hopped up on raspberry ripple; tripping on mint chip. So high you'd need a stepladder just to check their diapers.

Susan had the crowd in the palm of her hand as she reeled off one hit after another. *Old McDonald. Twinkle Twinkle Little Star...* They just don't write songs like these any more. The children were dancing in the aisles and stomping on their chairs, and many played along on whatever instrument was handy; it didn't matter. One little boy duck-walked the floor like Chuck Berry as he wailed away in a free-jazz ecstasy on a one-stringed ukulele. He didn't even bother to stop when the songs ended.

The kids shouted out requests like drunks at a piano bar, and Susan did not let them down. A rousing chorus of "The Wheels On The Bus Go 'Round and 'Round" had the joint jumping, and the quick segue into "Itsy-Bitsy Spider" brought the house down with its synchronized hand gestures.

A hush fell over the crowd as Susan paused to tune her guitar, and a three year-old boy named Gus took the stage to sing *I've Been Working On The Railroad*. Although heavily prompted by his mother at the back of the room, Gus got off to a rocky start in the first verse, but he came on strong during the out-chorus of "Dinah Wontcha Blow..." Pumped up by the seething energy of the toddler mosh pit in front of the stage, he gave it all he had before collapsing in a heap at the song's end.

The stage was set for the Big Finish, and there were squeals of delight as Susan launched into the opening strains of *The Hokey Pokey*. It was a real show-stopper, and when the house lights came up, the kids just about had to be poured into their strollers.

I highly recommend taking your young child to such a gathering. Group musical participation is critical to child development, especially if it provides an opportunity for you to eat ice cream.

GO FLY A KITE

A kite was once just a funny-shaped piece in Emma's jigsaw puzzle and a spokesman for the letter K in her alphabet books, but since last weekend's beach party, she is, at age sixteen months, a convert. She spent the entire time watching the kites fly, pointing skyward and yelling "Up!" lest there be any confusion.

Five days later, having lost all hope of any verbal interaction, which did not prominently feature the word "kite," I promised to take her out to get one. But where? When I was a kid, there were a couple of old fashioned local toy stores that always had kites.

Laboring under the temporary illusion that I am a part of mainstream society, I took Emma to Toys R Us®. They'll have kites, I thought. If anything, they'll have too many to choose from. We'll get lost in the Kite Annex of their building, and Emma will be traumatically over-stimulated by a kite display the size of a car dealership.

OK, now take a wild guess what they did not carry. To their credit, they did offer a large selection of many different kinds of flying toys, none of which were kites, but many of which had very lifelike depictions of Star Wars® characters.

I'll tell you what Toys R Us® did have, and that is Barbie® dolls. Hordes of them, staring us down from the shelves like bonsai Stepford Wives, sporting every conceivable costume, and festooned with the trappings of various far-flung scenarios that really try one's patience.

My favorite was the Golden Anniversary Barbie®. This thing was displayed in an elaborate glass case as though it was a diamond, or a salami or something, with a little engraved placard which read: "A Toys R Us® exclusive! In celebration of the Golden Anniversary of Toys R Us®, Barbie® wears a red AIDS awareness ribbon."

With a reverent moment of silence, I pondered this brilliant marketing concept: Barbie® celebrates corporate bloat by displaying her awareness of AIDS. How noble of her, to make this bold statement! I had no idea the doll community was so affected. That poor Golden Anniversary Barbie®, how many fellow Barbies®, Kens®, and Skippers® has she lost to this dreadful disease?

How could this happen? Certainly the absence of genitals rules out sexual contact. The obvious answer hit me like a ton of Legos®... it must be IV drugs. As a responsible journalist, I owe it to the public to get at the truth. Just not now.

Clearly, it was time to leave; I did not want Emma around this sort of bad influence. We had to buy something so they wouldn't think we were total deadbeats. At the bargain rack I was tempted by the "Official Military" play set which featured two hand grenades and a combat knife, figuring at least we could fight our way out of the Barbie® section. Instead I selected a cheap pail-and-shovel set for our next beach trip. $1.99, with no licensed character graphics. The cashier gave me that Lousy Cheapskate Glare®, but I thought Hey, if she doesn't like it, she can go fly a kite.

DISCIPLINE IS A PIECE OF CAKE

As your child rounds the corner from babyhood into toddlerhood, you must be prepared for her specific, long-term memory to lock in at any moment, which means that it's time to practice what you preach. You are running out of the days when you can smoke a foot-long cigar and say "Look, Sweetheart, Daddy's eating a loaf of wheat bread!"

You must start modeling good eating habits. This is tougher than you might think. Remember, as an adult you have earned the right to cram an entire bag of grease-infused, salt 'n vinegar flavored kettle chips down your sorry trap at the slightest hint of frustration, whereas babies enjoy no such liberties. Don't rub it in. Do the responsible thing: hide the chips, and gorge yourself behind a locked door.

This raises the larger question of sweets; specifically, should you allow sweets to be a part of your baby's diet, and if you do, what size crowbar should you use to pry the seventh consecutive Twinkie from her hand?

I found a web site with facts and figures about candy and chocolate, and, thanks to the candy manufacturers and distributors who sponsored it, was pleasantly surprised to learn that candy is a part of a sensible diet, and that chocolate is not habit-forming. Now here's the big shocker: It turns out that moderation is the key, which is like saying guns are perfectly safe as long as they never get pointed at anyone.

Which is precisely the problem when it comes to toddlers. They have as much sense of restraint as Genghis Khan. An adult has the maturity to stop eating ice cream when the half gallon is gone, while a toddler will demand that you produce another one right now, front and center.

As the only non-adult at a birthday party the other night, Emma was cruising along until the sudden, unexplained appearance of a German Chocolate Cake. As she watched six adults worship it as though it were an intelligent being from another galaxy before lining up obediently for slices, Emma understood that she was in the presence of a holy object. She would not be denied this experience.

The difficulty came after she had consumed perhaps one third of her body weight in cake while showing no signs of slowing down. We put it away but she suspected it was still somewhere on the property and asked for more.

It did not make any sense to her that fellow humans would choose to put a stop to the Good Thing.

At eighteen months of age, she knows quite a few words, and "cake" is certainly among them. She put her face an inch from mine and spoke as though trying to make herself understood to an exceptionally dense person with eighty, maybe ninety percent hearing loss. "Cake!... Cake!" Mildly irritated amusement, giving way to wild-eyed exasperation, trying to get it through my thick skull. "What part of 'CAKE' don't you understand?"

Later, after she fell asleep, I tried not to feel like a lying, treacherous pig as I had seconds.

GO WITH THE FLOW

If the Homedaddy expects to care for a breastfed baby when Mommy returns to work, she'll have to harvest some milk ahead of time to put up in the fridge. "Express" is the word they use in the Parenting business when they speak of this, although "pump" is what they mean. You can get a cheap hand pump that looks like something you'd use to inflate a volleyball, and is about as breast-friendly. If you are yuppie slime you will no doubt purchase the luxury package, featuring an electric double pump system and a calfskin carrying case.

The top-of-the-line rig looks like a cross between a Gucci handbag and a kidney dialysis machine. It straps right onto Mom's chest and allows her to "express" from both sides while keeping the hands free to make conference calls, sign documents, and lay off thousands of employees. This is a high-horsepower unit, designed for Executive Mom's need for instant results. Be careful: fourth gear is strong enough to suck crude oil deposits out of a dry lake bed. Remember ladies, always start the unit on low power unless you want your entire torso yanked up the intake tube. Important safety tip.

Since Emma never took to the bottle during her first year, I became something of a sippy-cup expert. They come in two basic varieties; free-flowing and no-spill. The free-flowing kind is great for keeping all clothing and porous household surfaces saturated at all times. The spill-proof kind, on the other hand, work too well. Some of them wouldn't spill a drop into your mouth even if you sucked hard enough to pull your molars out of their sockets.

I became encouraged recently when Emma took a renewed interest in the bottle. The only problem was that the nipples we had from a year ago don't flow fast enough to give her a good drink. It was killing the momentum; she'd yell for the bottle, I'd fetch it, and she'd take a couple of low-yield pulls before throwing it down in frustration.

I went shopping for new nipples but they only come in 2 sizes, "Newborn" and medium, which was the size we were already using at home. Julia's mother told us that Julia had the same problem as a baby. Her solution had been to heat a crochet hook, which is like a thin knitting needle, over a flame and use it to poke a bigger hole. She also reminded me that she had sent us this very implement, something of a family heirloom, some time ago... and I suddenly flashed on that little flame-blackened tool sitting in the bottom of the kitchen junk drawer.

Ten minutes later, the crochet hook had worked its magic. Emma was chugging away like a fraternity pledge with enough concentration to provide me with a rare moment of reflection. Back when I agreed to be a Homedaddy, I knew it would entail major lifestyle changes. I just never imagined I'd have to pierce my nipples.

SPARE THE CRIB, SPOIL THE CHILD?

Those in favor of early crib-training claim that a baby who is allowed to stay in bed with the parents will turn into an utterly dependent, chicken-livered, quivering lump of Jell-O who will be unable to choose between Coke and Pepsi. Conversely, those who defend the practice of sharing the family bed feel that a baby forced into early independence can spiral down into a lifetime of violence, obsession, and country line dancing in a never-ending struggle to fill the unmet needs of infancy.

Besides the psychological arguments, there are practical considerations. If you breastfeed, it is easier to feed a baby lying next to you than one lying in another room unless you have a truly unusual physique, or unless you are mechanically inclined and have a good supply of aquarium pumps and rubber tubing.

On the other hand, your best-laid plans to share the bed may get scotched by Junior's sleeping habits. Imagine the bliss of new parenthood shattered by the grisly discovery that Baby is an incorrigible blanket hog, or that she snores like a wildebeest with a sinus infection.

The worst candidate for group-sleeping is the "Hair-Trigger Sprawler." This is the baby who takes up an unreasonable amount of the bed's total surface area, and who wakes up screaming at the slightest nudge. Even you ultra-progressive touchy-feely parents might think twice after a few nights scrunched on your side along the outer four inches of the mattress with your face mashed painfully against a stuffed animal, grudgingly sacrificing your requirement to breathe from both nostrils, while struggling to ease the cramp in your hamstring by not thinking about it.

No matter what the sleeping arrangement, you need to establish a bedtime routine. Rather than yank her out of some pleasant evening activity such as pulverizing crayons with a meat tenderizer, try planning ahead a little. Get her used to a gentle and familiar sequence: putting on jammies, brushing teeth, and giggling hysterically while being chased around the house before being dragged off to bed in a screaming rage of over-stimulation.

Reading a bedtime story is also recommended. We tried a book of nursery rhymes, and although Emma enjoyed the singsong cadences, I was reminded of the old familiar brutality of the storybook world, with its random acts of cruelty and senseless acts of ugliness: Ladybug, ladybug, fly away home, your house is on fire and your children are gone... She whipped them all soundly and put them to bed... Ding dong dell, pussy's in the well... She cut off their tails with a carving knife... Jack fell down and broke his crown... Cripes, what a horror show. I had nightmares, but Emma slept like a rock. She's still young enough to know that all the bad stuff is make-believe.

SHOPPING WITH BABY:
NOT FOR THE TIMID

You aspiring Homedaddies, and Mommies, for that matter, are going to spend a great deal of your time grocery shopping. I try to stick to our little local market, since it provides a distinct advantage in atmosphere. This hit home the other day when Emma and I took a detour to visit the Jumbo Corporate Supermarket, the name of which I will not mention except to say that it implies that you may not be safe shopping elsewhere.

The real reason we were there was to deposit a check, since my bank maintains an ATM station right there next to a very attractive salami display. Once inside, I decided to take a spin around, strictly for research purposes.

It seemed that every child in the place seemed to have an incurable case of the Grabbies. They were snatching up gaudily-packaged products as fast as the moms could pry them loose and slam them angrily back onto the shelves.

This little scenario was being played out all over the store: Children grabbing things, and parents saying "NO!" as if training a deaf spaniel, often adding "Don't grab!" while ripping the item out of the child's grasp.

Emma got right into the groove, making a smooth, one-handed snag of a package of cookies as we rounded a corner. They were located so conveniently for the shopping cart kiddy seat, all she really had to do was stick out her hand. I took her out of the seat and let her walk, and she went straight for the ground-level stuff. I then tried carrying her, but she wriggled in my arms like a ferret on speed.

All I had picked up so far was some kitchen trash bags, but it was time to get out of there. Eighteen checkout lanes, two of them open, and ten people in line at each one. We fulfilled our civic duty by getting in line and scanning the magazines while the bozo in front tried repeatedly to buy his groceries with an expired library card. When an additional cashier, having finally finished her cigarette out in the parking lot, offered to help "the next person in line," Emma and I stayed put and watched four other shoppers duke it out.

Supermarket magazines feature articles mostly about losing weight and having better sex, and they share a display rack with enough candy to introduce Halloween to China. "10 Tips For Dynamite Sex," brays a typical headline, with a picture of a woman so skinny she has to jump around in the shower to get wet. "Make Him Think He's Having Better Sex!" "Lose 20 Pounds in 20 Minutes!" "Be A Totally Different Person!"

When you eventually reach the cashier, your purchase is double-bagged in plastic, even if all you are buying is plastic bags. It is an appropriate ending to a completely absurd experience, even though most people consider it the most normal thing in the world.

As much as I dread having to explain all this to Emma some day, I have an even greater fear that she'll think it makes perfect sense.

FUNNY BUSINESS

While staying abreast of world affairs by scanning the magazine rack, a patently ridiculous headline caught my eye: "Get Happy! Why Giggling Is Time Well Spent." Not that I have anything against this practice— what I do in the privacy of my own home is no on else's business— it just never occurred to me to write an article glorifying it

Of course this was a parenting magazine; one of those glossy jobs subsidized by the disposable diaper industry. I bought it just for this feature, which makes the outrageous claim that children enjoy and benefit from humor (wow, who knew?). The high-powered academic types who contributed all agree that children who laugh a lot have a good start in life. I'd like to pit these guys in a wire cage tag-team no-rules match against my elementary school teachers, who had different ideas.

Furthermore, the article says that children need parental support for their humor. On this point I agree, although I would note that an appreciation of slapstick and a stomach for repetition will serve you well. Unless you can agree that a dog wearing a banana peel for a wig is funny not once, but every two minutes for a three week run, you are going to be in for some tough sledding.

It is pointless to analyze the appeal of slapstick humor; so pointless, in fact, that many academic authorities have devoted their careers to it.

According to Amelia Klein, Ed.D. and associate professor of early childhood education, children love physical humor because it "reflects their attempts to master walking and moving about." Oh yeah, right. As if young children have ever been known to take a philosophical view of their own failings. I'd say the real reason they like it is because they like seeing someone else fall down for a change.

For another brilliant analysis, we are introduced to Paul McGhee, Ph.D., a developmental psychologist who claims that "Children have an innate desire to play with reality and to rearrange it." Sounds like the these children have futures in bioengineering. Dr. McGhee is also described as an "authority on humor who has written eleven books on the subject." Eleven books de-constructing humor... now there's a party guest from hell. Wouldn't you just love to hear him tell a joke.

I say it all boils down to the fact that it's funny to see someone fall down smack on their wallet, as long as there's no liability issue. True, there are degrees of subtlety. It may not be so funny seeing someone bump his head (unless he is a salesman), but the very same action accompanied by a well-synchronized sound effect of a hammer striking an anvil can be pure poetry.

In any case, you should encourage your child's sense of humor on his own level. So my advice to all of you new and aspiring Homedaddies is to get your hands on all of the Three Stooges episodes you can. Study them carefully, even if you don't enjoy it... although I can't imagine what sort of man wouldn't.

THE TWO FACES OF HOMEDADDY

It is true, being a Homedaddy is the greatest calling a man could have, offering rewards far beyond anything found in the more traditional male employment venues. However, before you get lost in an advertising-induced haze of Kodak-Hallmark-Nabisco-Proctor & Gamble imagery, you must be prepared to face the Dark Side.

For every slow motion, soft focus close-up of your child hugging you as the morning light streams through the kitchen window, while on the sound track the orchestra's string section swells and resolves with that heavenly major chord, you can be sure that your day will also hold the Anti-Moment, when your child stares at you with the horrible realization that you are a double agent, conspiring to bring betrayal and pain.

It is so cute when Baby is old enough to eat peanut butter and jelly, and even cuter when she can hold onto a hunk of sandwich and take bites on her own schedule. This is something you have been encouraging for weeks, and now you swell with pride at this awesome display of self-sufficiency. As you heap on enough praise to make Bill Gates blush, you notice that she has taken too many consecutive bites, and you can see a huge glob of it in there as she desperately tries to swallow.

Now she's panicking, and she doesn't want a drink of water or milk or juice to help wash it down, and you have to stick a finger in there and pull some of it off the roof of her mouth, but now this is bigger than peanut butter; it is a power struggle and a personal respect issue; a referendum on her self-esteem and a violation of her personal space. Never mind that all you want to do is let her eat her sandwich in peace without being stalked by the Specter of Death by Choking. A minute ago you said she was a big girl, and now you're going to pin her arms down while you stick a finger in her mouth? You have exposed your true self, you two-faced thug.

Another example: Babies shouldn't drink soda pop, so when she demands a drink of yours, you are firm and gentle, and above all, consistent (How about some juice?), but she still goes to pieces (No, you idiot, I do not want juice). To the horror of authors of parenting books, you ignore the very boundaries you set only moments before and concede a sip, but by now she's mad, and she's really going to show you by taking a humongous gulp. She's literally leaping at the nearly-full can as you try to lower it slowly to her mouth, and this starts a momentary tug of war, which she wins by virtue of the wailing noise way back in her throat. You stop pulling on the can, but the sudden lack of tension as she gives one final yank causes it to slightly bonk into her front teeth. It also causes some soda to slosh into her mouth at the exact moment that she gives a little gasp, so that she inhales it, which makes her cough and choke and spit soda all over both of you. When she gets her breath back enough to start crying, she fixes you with a glare that accuses you of punching her in the mouth, throwing soda in her face, and trying to choke her just to teach her some twisted daddy power-trip lesson. Sometimes you just can't win.

The bad news is that this happens on a daily basis. The good news is that children usually get over it and move on rather quickly. The real question is: Can you?

HALLOWEEN FOR BEGINNERS

It's Halloween time, so you Homedaddies will have some explaining to do. Very young children are confused when a neighbor converts his front yard to a makeshift cemetery, or hangs a bunch of ghosts and skeletons in the trees, or buys a bag of decorative fake cobwebs when his house already has plenty of real ones.

With Halloween, as with all other aspects of Little Kid Culture, it's important to keep things on the warm 'n fuzzy side. The "gross-out" concept of costume design is strictly off-limits. Do not dress your baby up as a severed head, a blood-drooling vampire child, or a wolverine attack victim. Also, avoid all "high concept" costumes; everyone knows it's just you having your own private chuckle. No one's going to believe that she begged to go as the Dancing Dwarf from the *Twin Peaks* dream sequences, or a fugitive drumstick on the run from Colonel Sanders.

I wanted to get Emma her first Halloween costume, but I didn't want to take her to one of those Halloween stores and expose her to twenty thousand square feet of severed rubber limbs, plastic medieval weapons, and injection-molded monster faces more realistic than most nose jobs. I could never explain to her satisfaction how "Scary," a well-known bad thing, can, in this case, also be "Fun," which is "Good." I'm still trying to get her to agree that eating paint is "bad."

I went alone to peruse the merchandise and select her costume, and after much deliberation (five minutes) I went with a proven winner: the Fuzzy White Bunny Suit, made of 100% low-grade spun polyester threads. Non-flammable, if the label is to be believed, although I suspect it would melt like a hairball if you left it in your car on a hot day.

The current conventional wisdom says that you should give young children some time to get used to their costumes. Like wrestling fans, they are rendered unstable by the inability to discern between "real" and "pretend." Some kids don't react so well to the sudden revelation that everything they've learned so far was just a big mistake, and that from now on they are, in fact, a rabbit.

As luck would have it, Emma loved her bunny suit and began to wear it around the house, which gave rise to a rather fascinating discovery: The

spun polyester fabric, in addition to being hot and itchy, also attracts dog hair so powerfully that you can see it flying in from other rooms to attach itself to the suit. Never mind what all that dog hair is doing in our house in the first place.

After two washing machine cycles failed to remove the dog hair, I remembered the Miracle Pet Hair Vacuum Attachment, acquired once upon a time and stored in the attic after one attempted use. Applying it to the bunny suit resulted in another amazing household discovery: The costume picks up dog hair better than the Miracle Pet Hair Vacuum Attachment.

It's a good thing Emma will soon be too big for this costume, because I can hardly wait to try it out on the rug. Meanwhile, I tossed the vacuum attachment out in the front yard. It makes a pretty good tombstone.

A NIGHT ON THE TOWN

Brand-new, first-time parents bring their newborn to a restaurant with enough food and gear to tide the Donner Party over till the spring thaw. Baby snoozes with a Buddha's peaceful countenance as perfect strangers linger at the table to heap on the praise and admiration. What a relaxed baby! So well behaved! So comfortable around strangers!

It's easy for new parents to get cocky, even if the offspring is still too young to know that she's even left the house. This is a snap, the parents think. Jeez, if she's already this comfortable in a restaurant, just think, in another year or two she'll be ordering the wine.

Veteran parents, having learned that things get tougher before they get easier, are amused by such hubris. Toddlers are less popular with the general public than infants. They are like the teenagers of the little kid world, thrilled by the prospect of rebellion against parents while remaining totally reliant upon them. They are physically able to cause serious trouble and sufficiently lacking in judgement to actually do it. They are capable of exhibiting pure beauty and senseless evil in the same moment. They also go through frequent phases of refusing to eat anything except goldfish crackers.

From about four months till around one year of age, you can strap a baby into a restaurant high chair for major spans of time (10 minutes, even), but the average toddler can undo those plastic seat belt clasps faster than Houdini. If this fails to get a rise, he'll learn to push against the table with both feet, tipping the entire high chair over backwards and causing both parents leap to their feet as though receiving an unexpected B12 shot in a crowded public place.

Dining out gets more expensive when your child is old enough to refuse to be fed scraps from grown-ups' plates, and it becomes necessary to order from a Kid's Menu which offers one-tenth the food for a mere eighty percent of the regular price. When ordering, stick to meals containing honey, lemon, raw egg, or beer, since these things are said to be good for the hair, and most very young children will rub most of it there anyway.

Even under optimum conditions, you can expect to create a significant mess. The last time we took Emma to our favorite Mexican restaurant, we ordered an extra side of rice. She got busy with her spoon and the whole thing was gone in minutes. I was thoroughly impressed with her appetite as well as her dexterity until I lifted her from the high chair and saw the entire serving fall from the folds of her clothes onto the floor. If you ever want to visit the same place twice you'd better be a big tipper.

Restaurants should really provide a special rubber room for families with toddlers. It would allow the Little One to career at will without the usual risk of skull fracture; plus, the room could be quickly hosed down after each family. And while they're at it, they could put side orders of goldfish crackers on the menu.

THE GOLDFISH STANDARD

Of all the tons of material written about the Y2K® Crisis®, there was no mention of the potentially devastating impact on the Homedaddy Industry. Parents faced a very real danger of being unable to provide the essentials of life for their small children, and by this I am obviously referring to Pepperidge Farm™ Goldfish® Crackers.

Although most experts agreed that you should have enough cash on hand for a month's supply of Goldfish® (about $3,000), there are others who said that simply having some extra coin laying around the house might not solve your problems if the grocery stores couldn't do business as usual. These people were afraid that the cash registers would all be going off like slot machines, so they wouldn't be able to take your money even if you tried to give it to them, although personally, I've never lost any sleep over the lack of anyone's willingness to take my money, broken cash register or no.

Nonetheless, I was relieved to learn that it was a non-issue according to another group of Y2K analysts who had their knickers in a knot just because they thought the country's trucking, shipping, and railroad schedules were controlled by a massive and hopelessly non-compliant network of ancient, wood-burning computers, all of which would go paws-up on January 1. So don't worry about cash registers, said this group, because your local store won't have any more Goldfish® crackers in stock anyway.

A troubling notion, but fortunately, there was another layer of theorists assuring us that the so-called concern about transportation control systems was nothing but alarmist tripe anyway, since the Y2K bug would cause such disruption in the oil business that there wouldn't be any gasoline anyhow. See? No sense worrying about some stupid trucking schedule. What a relief!

But what about the gasoline? Not a problem, according to yet another faction who were convinced that large scale food manufacturers would be shut down anyway due to their own internal computer failures. With nothing to ship, they wouldn't be needing much fuel. Furthermore, the shutdown of food production facilities would be immaterial, once disruption in farming and chemical industries would interrupt supplies of enriched flour. They wouldn't be making those dastardly little nuggets in the first place.

Where were we to go from here? Well, there was always that other charming group of optimists who suggested we should immediately start learning to be a blacksmith or a cobbler, because at 12:01 AM on 1/1/00, all of the world's computers would emit a little puff of smoke and make a cuckoo clock noise, and before you can say "non-compliant" we'd all be bounced right back to the Middle Ages.

So forget about hoarding cash. The smart Homedaddy at the turn of the millennium should instead stockpile several tons of Goldfish® crackers, since they would clearly be the commodity of the future.

TAKE THE HOMEDADDY QUIZ

Before you make the decision to enter the booming Homedaddy Industry, take a few moments and test your aptitude.

How do you react to a piercing scream emitted inches from your ear?
   a Take it in stride
   b Jump out of your seat
   c Drop your beer
   d Draw your gun

What is your reaction to being suddenly awakened in the middle of the night?
   a concern
   b annoyance
   c rage
   d earplugs

What do you consider to be an acceptable level of background noise?
   a The pitter-patter of little feet, a barking dog, the *Teletubbies* theme song on the TV, a phone ringing, knocking at the door, some random screaming and crying, and two different radios tuned to different stations at high volume,
   b Burl Ives nursery rhyme albums and the drone of an old washing machine,
   c books on tape, or
   d nothing at all, just peace and quiet.

Your idea of a nice day at home is:
   a Sorting laundry and running a load of whites,
   b reading the collected works of Dr. Seuss,
   c relax and watch a ball game, or
   d nothing at all, just peace and quiet.

You are trying to encourage your baby to eat a creamed, processed, spinach-derived product. You perform a detailed pantomime depicting ingestion of same, and the resulting profound yummy sensation in the tummy region. Baby's resolve weakens for a moment and he actually eats a spoonful. Your reaction is to:

   a offer praise and encouragement,

   b sneak the next bite in as soon as possible, before the taste buds have a chance to check in with the brain,

   c put your hands on your hips and say "There, now that didn't kill you did it?"

   d laugh and point while yelling "He fell for it!"

Score 20 points for each *"a"* answer, 10 points for each *"b,"* 5 points for each *"c"* and zero points for each *"d"* answer.

How do you stack up?

Over 80: Homedaddy Hall of Fame material. You didn't have time for this quiz because you are busy making homemade mint jelly and drying organic tomatoes for the winter and singing the alphabet song and talking on the phone and demonstrating the hokey pokey and scrubbing out the diaper pail and teaching your child how to make model dinosaurs out of discarded aluminum foil. You make Martha Stewart look like trailer trash. When you take the baby out for a walk you gather a wildflower bouquet to arrange in the entry hall to give your wife a little welcome-home surprise before giving her a full body massage, during which you lull the baby to sleep with ethnic nursery rhymes from around the world sung in authentic dialects.

   70–80: go for it; you'll probably do fine

   60–70: could pull it off provided child is a complete angel

   50–60: marry someone who wants to be a full-time mom

   40–50: marry someone with grown children

   30–40: marry someone who wants to raise chinchillas

   20–30: don't get married

   10–20: don't ever have sex again

   0–10: don't leave it to chance; get a vasectomy

TWO THINGS ARE CERTAIN: DEATH AND TELETUBBIES

As the twentieth century drew to a close nothing could strike fear into the Homedaddy's heart as much as the phrase "It's time for Teletubbies," which in case you didn't know, is the slogan and opening line of a children's program on public television featuring a quartet of roly-poly terry cloth androids with antennae on their heads and video screens set into their stomachs. And these are their more endearing qualities.

Besides being the darlings of the Under-Two Set, the Teletubbies enjoyed instant notoriety when they drew the attention of that fine arbiter of public taste, the Rev. Jerry Falwell. It seems that the largest Teletubby, who performs under the name of Tinky-Winky, was (according to Falwell) actually a homosexual role model. This attempted character assassination on a puppet made out of a purple dishrag immediately caught the attention of the American public, which correctly identified this behavior as absurd, even for Falwell.

So, naturally, he did the honorable thing and claimed he'd been misunderstood, and proved it by hooking up with Tinky-Winky himself for a publicity photo of the two of them sharing a nice cold beer at a Hooters Restaurant. It was a close call for Falwell, but as they say in the Public Relations business, it was nothing that wouldn't hose off.

When Emma was born I swore I'd never allow the Teletubbies into my house, but of course that was before she was able to express herself. She truly enjoys them, and that is enough to make me turn the other cheek even though I can feel myself dropping an IQ point for every minute that they are on my television set.

Recently, as Julia and I faced domestic pressures of various kinds, the Teletubbies became my personal scapegoats. I cursed them for invading my dreams, mocking my goals, and altering global weather patterns. I entertained private fantasies of burning them in effigy and sticking pins into them like voodoo dolls.

In the middle of my self-centered blame-fest, we received the news on Thanksgiving Day that my sister had died. She lived in Paris, France with her husband and two young children, and had been fighting cancer for about two years.

It wasn't practical for all of us to go, and I traveled to Paris alone in a state of shock, grief, and confusion. My mind swirled with thoughts and feelings both sane and otherwise, and at one point I remember thinking, at least I'll have a few days rest from those blasted Teletubbies. The relief was short-lived; the awareness that I was thinking of my own petty comforts at such a time made me feel like a selfish pig.

By the time I landed I was silently screaming at myself to stop thinking about the Teletubbies and face the music, but once I left the airport, my grip on reality evaporated as I beheld giant billboards everywhere in Paris pitching the Teletubbies, complete with translated slogan: "C'est l'heure de Teletubbies!" I didn't know what to think. I still don't. I probably never will.

ASK HOMEDADDY: READERS SPEAK OUT

Dear Homedaddy,

I am trying to be consistent, just like the parenting books say, but I keep running into problems. Recently I convinced our 8-month-old son to eat his food by demonstrating that it smelled good. Later that day, while taking him for a walk in his stroller, I let him smell some roses which he then wanted to eat. In fact, he became extremely upset when I would not allow it, and no amount of explanation seems to satisfy him. He's been giving me dirty looks for the past three days. What should I do?

> Eager To Please
> Dry Fork, Iowa

Dear Eager,

Forget it. You are a hypocrite of the lowest order. Your son isn't fooled for a minute. Take a good long look at yourself.

Dear Homedaddy,

Personally, I work for a living like any self-respecting Real Man, but recently I took the day off to watch the kids just to see what all the hubbub is about. I was shocked and disgusted by the television shows kids are exposed to these days. Hour after hour of PBS programs about fairness, diversity, and sharing. And if that wasn't enough, a furry purple dinosaur singing about his feelings, for Pete's sake. In my day, it was a treat to see a cartoon character drop an anvil from a tremendous height onto the skull of an adversary. But not anymore, no, nowadays they all have to have a group hug at the end and sing a song about love. It's no wonder this country's a mess!

I say, bring back the classic tales of survival.

> Blood and Guts
> Fort Benning, GA

Dear Blood and Guts,

I agree. I miss the cartoons of yore, and sometimes I still get the urge to settle a dispute by offering someone a stick of dynamite disguised as a cigar, although I rarely act on it. Those old cartoons were fun, but you have to admit they had a negative side. For many years I thought I could thwart a point-blank shotgun attack simply by sticking my fingers into the barrels, which would cause the gun to backfire in the face of the aggressor with no risk to me.

Dear Homedaddy,

My one-year-old son thinks that breaking wind is the funniest thing in the world. Whenever he does it, or worse yet, hears someone else do it, he laughs himself into a state which I could only describe as religious ecstasy. What can I do to teach him that this is a normal bodily function and not a source of entertainment?

> Aghast About Gas
> Portland, Oregon

Dear Aghast,

What do you mean, not a source of entertainment?

HOMEDADDY'S HOLIDAY VIDEO REVIEW

Back in the old days, before my high horse was sent off to the glue factory, I always thought that if I ever have a child, I'll shield her from the ravages of television. She'll meet her share of knuckleheads, creeps, and salesmen the minute she's old enough to step out of the house, so why bother turning on the tube before then?

For a little peace and quiet, that's why. Emma will be two years old in March, and you could say that my idealism has been tempered by practicality. She loves her Dr. Seuss videos, as well as a couple of others, and by now I am just relieved that she isn't watching reality TV.

It is a personal requirement of mine that her videos all contain some educational content; that way I can forgive myself for plunking her in front of the Idiot Box while I get lost in the hedonistic bliss of standing motionless and staring into a corner for a few minutes.

Even though small children love repetition and will watch the same video ten thousand times in a row, you must be prepared for the day when they suddenly demand something new. Fortunately or otherwise, there is no shortage of videos aimed at children, thus the burden falls to the discriminating parent to sort through the avalanche of advertising disguised as programming in the form of animated characters and fuzzy puppets. This week, Homedaddy reviews a few of the recent holiday offerings.

Humbug! It's The Teletubbies – The four lovable, fat-butted, terry cloth androids get caught up in a flurry of Christmas activities, including searching in vain for mall parking, waiting in line at the post office, and getting a ticket from a meter maid in a Santa hat. In a special musical number, little Po is visited by a magic star that teaches her to say "gimme."

Mickey's Christmas Tantrum – This video features your favorite Disney characters in a series of endearing short stories. Your child will learn, the fun way, that love, respect, and sharing might be important, but that all three of them plus twenty five cents will get you a replacement Christmas tree light bulb. This video also carries an important message for the parents of older kids: They will hate whatever you get them, so don't risk tarnishing their dreams by getting what they've asked for.

Barney's Fact-Finding Mission – The Valium-addled dinosaur and his pals travel to the North Pole to protest child labor conditions among the elves. In a madcap turn of events, they wind up going to work for Santa as his personal PR team after being offered sizable retainers and stock options. They stay on at the Pole through Christmas in order to attend Santa's legendary New Year's Eve party, only to be stranded there forever when the Y2K bug crashes the navigational equipment in their airplane.

Each of these are fine videos in their own right, with lovable characters and positive underlying messages your children will remember long after they have forgotten your name.

BABY SHOWER

Although most babies love bath time, there are some who hate having their hair washed. It's no big deal for infants sporting little or no hair, but by about two years of age, most toddlers are using whatever they've got to full advantage, as a receptacle for maple syrup.

When a toddler hates something, you'll know about it; in fact, everyone on your block will know about it. A recalcitrant toddler being subjected to shampoo by force will do his best to convince the neighbors that his toes are being lopped off with pruning shears. Given the acoustical properties of the average bathroom, you can expect some long-term hearing loss.

An aversion to hair-washing is regrettable. The dried syrup does make a certain fashion statement, in a low-rent mohawk sort of way, and although it is true that there is something vaguely comforting about having a baby that smells like a pancake breakfast, it only interferes with the olfactory cues essential to prompt diaper attention.

The only thing some babies hate more than being shampooed is waiting for you to take a shower. Unless you move a TV set into the bathroom, the duration of your shower will depend entirely on the child's mood.

A bored baby rapidly deteriorates into a panicked baby, which spells trouble. A panicked baby is a danger to himself and to society, even if your bathroom is "toddler compliant." It is necessary, while showering, to keep one's ears tuned to the slightest rumblings of discontent in order to finish up and get out before the kid goes off like an air raid siren and passing motorists call Child Protective Services.

You will learn to take faster showers than you ever thought possible, and no time-saving idea is too ridiculous. I personally recommend the use of a hand-held spray nozzle, which allows one to rinse the soap from one's nether regions much faster than would be possible under a standard shower spray, unless you stand on your head and bicycle your legs in the air, which, according to the Consumer Safety Bureau, is the number one cause of fatal bathroom accidents.

There are plenty of days when a shower is not in the cards at all. Since your hair will often look as though you spent the night in a vacant lot, it is advantageous to have a good supply of baseball caps on hand.

It is now common knowledge among the more enlightened folks that you can't get babies to do things your way through brute force, although it is still being attempted in many places. No, you have to be sneaky. Today's Homedaddy Tip: Don't put maple syrup on the pancakes. Use shampoo instead. The baby will get plenty of it worked nicely into the hair. Don't worry if she doesn't eat the pancakes. She's saving her appetite for goldfish crackers.

DRESS FOR SUCCESS, TODDLER STYLE

New research has shown that babies begin forming opinions in the womb, as early as six weeks after conception. By birth, they have fully-formed notions about how to be held, how to feed, and whether it's OK to wear white shoes after Labor Day.

By the time the child starts developing speech abilities, she'll be absolutely brimming over with opinions just waiting for a voice. Parenting books tell you that a good way to "empower" your child, as well as build her verbal skills, is to allow her to pick out clothing to wear. If you have ever done this you will recall the feeling of relief that your child is not dressing for a job interview.

Young children do not choose clothing at random, which would at least result in an occasional match. They play the individual favorites: polka dot pants, plaid shirt, Winnie-The-Pooh hat, one cowboy boot and one rubber beach sandal. Efforts to attenuate these decisions will result in disaster; do not try.

Theoretically, if you indulge them in this practice early, they'll eventually get the hang of it, while conversely, children who are not allowed to go through this process will suffer the consequences as adults. It has not traditionally been considered important to let young boys pick out their clothes, which explains why most bachelors have the fashion sense of two-year-olds.

Important note: Do not urge your child to pick out clothing if he shows no interest in doing so. The very worst thing you can do is to hold up each piece of clothing separately and say "How about this?" unless it is your intention never to leave the room. The "No" Reflex will engage, even if the child really doesn't give a fig either way.

Most children outgrow this trait, thanks to a recessive gene that kicks in somewhere down the line. Children lacking this gene become stuck at this stage of emotional development and often become corporate middle managers or studio executives.

I let Emma choose her own outfits as often as possible, with the result that sometimes she looks like a survivor of a bomb attack in a thrift store. She made quite an entrance to the toney women's boutique where we recently shopped for Julia's birthday gift, and her fashion statement did not go unnoticed by the snooty saleswoman who probably owned an embroidered toilet paper "cozy" to match the trim on her bathroom curtains. As Actress Elsa Lanchester once said about Maureen O'Hara, "She looked as though butter wouldn't melt in her mouth... or anywhere else." So palpable was her scorn that I felt obligated to acknowledge the source of our socio-retail friction.

"Ha, ha," I joked, stroking my five-day stubble and cocking an eyebrow towards Emma. "Guess who insisted on choosing her clothes today!"

The woman raised a plucked eyebrow.

"Her daddy?"

After a short but ugly silence, my muttered explanations sounded like a confession. I'd like to say we took our business elsewhere but we found something really nice.

A GRAIN OF SALT GOES A LONG WAY

Even the casual observer of early childhood development knows there are no hard and fast rules. One child might learn the alphabet by adding one letter a year until he achieves a closure of sorts at the age of 26, while another might awaken one fine day at the ripe old age of eighteen months and calmly mention that he'd like to try eating cereal with a fork one time, just to see what it feels like.

The ability to utter words and phrases should never be confused with the ability to comprehend and communicate complex ideas, especially during an election year. Very young children, like politicians, can say things which at first can sound logical, or even startling, until one considers the source.

A woman we knew, according to my family's folklore, was approached one day by her novice talker. Clearly puzzled, the tot struggled to find the right words before blurting "What good is it?"

A tough question, no matter how you slice it. The mother wanted to establish some context, but the best she could manage was a feeble "What do you mean? What good is what?"

"What good is it? What good is it?" The tyke was getting his hackles up. He was in no mood to mince words; he wanted some straight answers and he wanted them now. The mother began to panic; she was sitting on a powder keg. The kid barely knew his colors but had apparently decided it was time to get down to brass tacks. She wished she had a decent answer.

She kept hedging, but he refused to parse the question. He was on to something and he knew it, and no grown-up, not even Mommy, was going to throw it out on a technicality. He began to repeat the query in an endless loop, ramping up the intensity until at last came the inevitable crash. She could hardly begrudge him the tantrum, since this very question had brought her to similar results more times than she cared to admit.

When he calmed down and realized his mother was doing her best, he finally elaborated: "Sometimes it's good morning and sometimes it's good night... what good is it now?"

Indeed, what good is it?

You have to take it all, as they say, with a grain of salt. Emma is almost two years old. The other day she grabbed my face, looked me in the eyes, and delivered the line with heart-stopping sincerity: "So sweet Papa." I was blissfully destroyed. Up till this point I had been strictly second fiddle; a cheesy opening act trying to warm up the crowd till Mommy comes home. Now, finally, my just reward.

An hour later she sat on my lap as I checked my E-mail. Pointing at the monitor, she looked me in the eye once again and intoned: "So sweet computer." With so many grains of salt in my daily diet it's no wonder I'm hyper-tense.

CHASING THE SANDMAN

Childless friends often ask how life has changed since we became parents. As I sit here nodding off at the keyboard, struggling to stay awake through the wee hours, inspiration comes to me: I want to go to sleep.

Emma still shares our bedroom, and although she has her own small bed, she spends about half the time in ours. She is getting used to falling asleep in her own bed, but when she wakes during the night we just reel her in.

Her ability to fall asleep in her own bed is still intermittent. Our technique in recent days has been for me to try first, and if I fail, to bring in the Closer. That would be Julia.

I usually read Emma some books before turning out the light, and then I try a story or two. If the story is boring enough, she'll fall asleep in the middle of it. I've learned the hard way to allow stories to trail off into silence rather than concluding them. Even when she has already begun to snore lightly, just hearing the phrase "The End" will cause her to open her eyes and say "'Nother one."

I've learned how to make stories double back on themselves and blend into one another. Emma will grow up thinking that *Goldilocks and The Three Little Bears, The Three Billy Goats Gruff, The Ugly Duckling and Tp0------ ------------nmhe Princess and the Pea* are nothing but one long, rambling tale full of gratuitous plot changes.

Another technique is to insert detail into stories to draw them out. Some of my versions of Goldilocks include sidebar descriptions of the rooms in the home of the Three Bears. Emma knows what magazines they subscribe to, what kind of material their curtains are made of, and how many sets of Daddy Bear's car keys are lost under the sofa cushions.

Eventually, she will go to sleep, and although she sleeps soundly most of the time, there are still enough interruptions to ensure that Julia and I still both walk around like zombies half the time, which is actually kind of helpful for me since a normal day can include reading the same "Winkie the Weasel" book a dozen times.

Permanent insomnia can set in after so many months of interrupted sleep. Once the body gets trained to wake up every few hours, it's tough to get back to normal patterns.

The trick is knowing how to get back to sleep quickly, which is no small feat if you are a worrier like me. The other night I tried counting sheep, and after I reached about three thousand, I stayed up another two hours wondering where the hell I was going to keep them all.

SELLING THE DREAM

Between a nasty cold, teething pain, and a stressful week at home, Emma's last few nights have been characterized by fevers, coughing fits, and night terrors. With the lure of dreamland thusly diminished, she's been understandably reluctant to hit the hay. She holds out for a really good story; no more remakes of *Goldilocks and the Three Bears.*

I am always in the market for new bedtime stories, and having exhausted the traditional catalogue, will beg, borrow, or steal from any old source. The other night I began an improvised yarn about the Teletubbies, but she gave it the hook after the opening ten seconds. With a dismissive wave of the hand, she gave me a world-weary "No, Papa," letting me know that the Teletubbies are no longer hip. They are, like, so twentieth century.

She has a new favorite show called *Dragon Tales,* an animated ditty about two regular old earthling kids who visit "Dragonland" to play with their dragon friends. This is a show for preschoolers, so it has talking trees, lots of pastel colors, and very friendly dragons. They act just like little kids themselves and never experience sudden fits of fire-breathing rage where they reduce some innocent bystander into a steaming lump of charcoal. This is how I know the show isn't about real dragons.

This week's bedtime stories have been decidedly dragon-centric. I always try and work in a little incentive, like mentioning twenty or thirty times that you can only visit Dragonland if you are asleep, and furthermore, that once you fall asleep, the nice dragons from the TV show might come and invite you to play.

I tell these stories with mixed feelings because I know better. Anyone familiar with the classic old fairy tales knows not to fool around with dragons, unless you want to wind up blazing away like a cub scout's marshmallow. Still, I am willing to go along with the saccharine version if it helps achieve bedtime armistice.

Do something for me now, and you will get a reward later... the tried-and-true technique of politicians, evangelists, and diet mongers. Sure, it's a bill of goods, but it works on the toddlers; a man desperate for sleep can stoop

pretty low. If you're lucky, she'll dream the sweet dreams as advertised and you'll jump a few points in the approval ratings, and get a good night's sleep while you're at it.

This was not a good week for me to make promises of sweet dreams to Emma. Between her cold, her new teeth, and the New Hampshire primaries, there have been plenty of reasons to wake up screaming. I just hope it wasn't the dragons.

TANTRUMS AND STRESS

Learning to be a parent is not like learning anything else. You do not begin with lesson one and proceed in a linear fashion through lesson two and so on. Every day is lesson one.

Despite the scare tactics of birth class and horror stories from other parents, the early days are actually pretty easy. It's just a matter of losing a lot of sleep and worrying about the future. All you really have to do is provide unconditional love, which is easy. Your job as parents is to pour it on, to wait on that baby hand and foot and let her know that you are there to see

to her slightest need. The experts will tell you that you simply cannot spoil a newborn baby, although you should try.

Now flash-forward about eighteen months. All of your how-to books about infant care are in cardboard boxes in the garage awaiting a yard sale or another pregnancy, whichever comes first. You now own a new set of instruction books for toddler care that spend a great many chapters talking about "establishing boundaries," a term reminiscent of international diplomacy and dog obedience training.

How appropriate.

Much has been written about the trials and tribulations of toddlerhood. The child is learning that she is a separate entity, that she can make decisions of her own, and that by screaming at a certain frequency she can cause toast to appear at the breakfast table minus the crusts.

A recent study suggests that the so-called "Terrible Twos" have less to do with a child's personality than with the stress level of the parents. Talk about a feedback loop.

Of course, the experts weigh in with some useful advice, as usual. Jay Belsky, a professor of Human Development and Family Studies at Penn State, suggests that parents can minimize tantrums by recognizing the child's need for independence. Instead of just saying "No," Belsky explains, the more sensitive parent elaborates: "No, you can't climb on that, you'll hurt yourself."

This guy has apparently never met a two-year-old, which is not surprising since there are very few of them enrolled at Penn State.

Once a tantrum has begun there are several different approaches. Although some knuckleheads still advocate spanking, the most common technique is known as the "Time Out," which is fine if your house has a rubber room where the enthusiastic youngster can flail away in good faith without risking serious injury.

Above all, keep your cool. The tantrum will play itself out, and the more relaxed you are afterwards, the less likely the tantrum will return, or so they tell us. And what exactly do the experts have to tell us about staying relaxed? Parenting expert Lynn M. Johnson suggests buying yourself a rose. "There's nothing like the smell and touch of real flowers," she notes.

She's right, you know. The last time I bought a fake one it made me feel so empty inside that Emma pitched a little fit just to show that she cared.

MEALS AND DEALS

In accordance with the Human Race® Employee Manual, when a baby reaches a certain stage of development, she is promoted to Toddler, a position with entirely new job duties. The Toddler Mission Statement, as quoted from the manual: "To realize that I am actually a distinct and separate human being in my own right, and not actually a piece of my mother that can detach and move around the room of my own accord, only to re-attach when the mood strikes."

The Toddler's job description calls for periods of refusal to cooperate with any activity suggested by a parent, the purpose being to determine which of these activities are essential to sustaining life. In the face of such tactics, parents must be very careful to pick the right battles. No point getting into a screaming tug-of-war over the choice of socks, only to run out of gas and get apathetic when she becomes curious about power tools.

Infants get upset at the drop of a hat but then get over it just as quickly. Toddlers are burdened with a longer attention span, and will hold a grudge for hours, if not decades. Suddenly, the parent finds that life is a series of negotiations. There are several popular models for negotiating with toddlers:

Authoritarian model: "Because I said so." A totally ineffective strategy unless you plan to rent out the spare room fourteen years from now.

Sports model: "I'll trade you this piece of zucchini now for a vegetable to be named later." Equally worthless. Toddlers are notorious for refusing to make good on these deals.

Confectionery model: A sugar-based reward system that provides a quick fix but lacks behavioral merit in the long term. A particularly bad choice at bedtime.

Seussian, also known as the "Green Eggs and Ham" model: Wearing the child down with endless variations on the theme until she relents. "Would you, could you with a goat, in a boat, with a fox, in a box, on a train in the rain..."

Remember, when negotiating, that you must always keep your word. If you say "one more bite," you'd better mean it, and if you say "one more bite then we'll have ice cream," you'd better not be yanking anyone's chain.

Never make an offer you are not prepared to honor, and stay on your toes; your child will catch on faster than you expect.

Last week, during a very healthy lunch that required much negotiating, Emma's interest lagged. She stared wistfully off into space and mumbled something like, "Onga pah..." Since she usually speaks very clearly, I wondered if she was feeling well. I prompted her: "What did you say? You want to go to the park?"

That was all it took. She snapped back to attention, looked me right in the eye and said, "OK."

Well, a deal's a deal. After a little while at the park she got hungry and we came home and finished lunch.

TACKLING THE TERRIBLE TWOS

Babies are so utterly helpless, so totally dependent on adult care, it is miraculous that human beings have persisted this long. Only the fact that parents think their offspring are unbelievably cute drives them to provide every last detail necessary for the survival of the infant, from adequate food and shelter to state-of-the-art stuffed animals.

Most people think babies are cute, but nature takes no chances. As a new parent gazes upon the newborn, some gland or another squirts about seven gallons of "Swoon Hormone" into the bloodstream, which drives the devotion level through the roof.

From a survival standpoint, parents eventually need to be jolted out of the Swoon Stage, otherwise, they'll forget to go back to work or take out the garbage and will instead spend every waking hour shooting pictures of the baby and spending the family nest egg on processing.

As usual, nature provides a mechanism, and parents mutter darkly to one another of something called "The Terrible Twos," which is that stage of development when your child begins to recognize and exploit the gaping holes in your moral and ethical fabric. It's also a time when the child no longer needs the same degree of doting care required by a newborn. It's a tough adjustment, but Mother Nature helps out by abruptly shutting off the supply of Swoon Hormone. It's like throwing a switch: One moment you think you're living on a Hallmark card, and the next thing you know you're taking orders from a 26-pound dictator.

Seeking advice, I searched the web for the phrase "terrible twos." The first thing I found was posted to a discussion group by someone named Tracey: "You have to convince him that you are stronger than he is. If he pulls at your arm while you're leading him, immediately turn him firmly in a small circle. Don't allow him to go back where he wants until he is finally walking straight and in control. It might take 10 circles, but hang in there, he will get fed up. If he tries to rear when you're leading, slap him sharply on nose and shout NO!"

This is barbaric, I thought, recoiling in disgust from the computer. I wouldn't even train an animal this way! I watched Emma as she hummed to herself and played with some building blocks, and I cringed to think of how some people handle their kids.

I decided to get back online and give this Tracey broad a piece of my mind.

I dashed off a scathing rebuttal and was about to send it when I realized that Tracey's advice was posted in a discussion group for horse trainers. I shut off the computer and settled down to play with Emma. My righteous parental wrath was a false alarm, but I'll be darned if it didn't trigger a little blast of Swoon Hormone.

NORMAL IN A CRAZY WORLD

If you want to succeed as a Homedaddy® you have to stay on top of all of the current professional literature, and that's not just reading Curious George several times a day. There are dozens of glossy parenting magazines and hundreds of web sites you must read hourly, in addition to scanning all the newspapers you can get your hands on.

Although the IRS will probably not accept your subscription to Highlights Magazine as a business deduction, do not be discouraged in your quest for knowledge as you navigate the welter of parenthood. Take care, however. Much of the information you will encounter is contradictory in nature.

In honor of Emma's rapidly approaching second birthday, I was reading up on toddler behavior and the so-called "Terrible Twos." A recent study conducted by SPLC (Serious People In Lab Coats) found that uncontrollably negative toddler behavior has less to do with the child's inherent temperament than with the stress and anxiety in the parents' lives.

To the frustrated parent, this may not come as the most helpful information.

Here's the scene: You're trying to leave the drugstore. Your child has latched onto the rotating sunglass rack and will not let go despite your coaxes, pleas, and bribes. Any attempt to budge her will topple the display. While reminding her that she has fourteen pairs of sunglasses at home, you gently begin to pry her little fingers loose, which causes her to emit a scream that makes Jimi Hendrix roll over in his grave and stick his fingers in his ears.

All eyes in the building turn toward you, and you know, in that instant, that everyone else has read this article, and as you stand there in judgment, your anxiety level spikes. Nice job. According to that study, you've just bought yourself another day of tantrums. Thanks a lot, Lab Coats.

Then there's the flip side. A front page article in Wednesday's San Jose Mercury News describes research showing that increasing numbers of preschoolers as young as age 2 are being treated with "behavior altering drugs," including stimulants, antidepressants, and antipsychotic drugs. See? It's not your fault after all!

Now, excuse me, but I thought 2-year-olds are lunatic by nature... oh, yeah, right, and also because their parents are hand-wringing, whimpering blobs of Jell-O. How naughty does a toddler have to be in order to qualify for a dose?

Children under age 2 were beyond the scope of the study. According to the article, certain computer limitations prohibited the study from including data on medication use in infants 1-year-old and younger. The constraints of a 2-digit field for date of birth made it impossible to distinguish those 1-year-old and younger from 100- and 101-year-olds. But honestly, how many 100-year-olds are being treated for hyperactivity?

I think the whole world is crazy. Toddlers are just starting to get a sense of it, so they act appropriately. Do yourself and your child a favor and don't read too much about parenting. Go outside and play instead.

PHOTOGRAPHIC MEMORY

Not that my memory was all that great to begin with, but now it's a lost cause. I bought some gingko biloba but I keep forgetting to take it.

When Emma was born, I set out with beginner's enthusiasm, determined to be the Super-Homedaddy®. I would plan and pack meticulously for the simplest of outings, with ample provisions of food, drink, extra clothing, diaper changing kit, blankets, books, toys, map, compass, and of course the camera, to

capture those precious moments that seem to occur every few seconds during the early months of Baby's life but then taper off.

Now, nearly two years down the road, Emma has wrestled me down to her level; we coexist on a sort of a "right now" basis. I have difficulty separating my train of rational thought from the rambling din of toddler life: Nursery rhymes, bedtime stories, and TV show jingles occupy chunks of my brain that used to be in charge of locating my car keys. It's been months since I could plan enough to bring the camera anywhere.

Truthfully, my brain has always been oddly selective. I retain a vast archive of pop culture detritus but it often takes me a minute to remember how old I am. I remember every word of the 1960's TV commercial jingle for the board game *Trouble*, (with the revolutionary "Pop-A-Matic" dice-rolling feature), but I don't remember the birth dates of immediate family members. Is this simply neural gymnastics or a cry for help?

I used to struggle for control but now I just sort of stay in the moment. My recent failures to pack elaborate snacks for outings is offset by the fact that the pockets of all of my clothes, Emma's clothes, plus the car and stroller seats are all lined with enough Goldfish cracker remnants to sustain an Everest expedition. Things generally work themselves out.

Well, mostly. I thought about bringing the camera when we took a walk down to the playground a few rainy days ago but by the time we left the house I had forgotten about it. A couple of things happened: While stumbling across the playground, Emma spontaneously discovered the joy of stomping in puddles. Dancing around, cackling with delight, making big splashes. Then the clouds shifted and a gigantic rainbow appeared, spanning the entire horizon, and, from my angle, perfectly framing Emma in her impromptu celebration. In my wishful arrogance I actually started reaching for the camera before remembering that I forgot.

I considered running home for it, but the clouds were already shifting and I didn't want to interrupt Emma's reverie. I tried to etch the scene into my brain. I really do have a photographic memory, I just forget to take the lens cap off sometimes.

I'm hedging my bets by telling as many people as possible. One of you can remind me of it, years from now when the only thing left rattling around in my mind is "Pop-A-Matic pops the dice, pop a six and you move twice…"

THE AMAZING TECHNICOLOR DREAMBAG

A parent's life is full of nonsense. You spend your entire adult life up to this point trying to create some personal context in a loopy world, cramming square pegs into round holes where necessary and resorting to prayer, meditation, exercise, or hedonism to drown out the cognitive dissonance.

You may have finally reached a place where most things, at least, make sense, while the rest of it gets lumped together in a brain file called "Everything Else." Then you have children, and as you enter into their world, your brain files get corrupted, and the contents of the "Everything Else" file gets scattered everywhere, imposing its absurd properties on the rest of life as you know it.

A young child's life takes place in an alternate reality where tiny plastic pigs and goats are not only living, breathing creatures, but can also communicate telepathically and are trusted advisors for any trip to the market. Applesauce is an effective nerve tonic when applied topically, and books must be confined to a hamper when they misbehave.

This netherworld of blurred boundaries and mixed metaphors flows outward from the child and overpowers all other humans in the household. Adult conversation, once the mainstay, has been reduced to nothing more than the need to spell the key words in sensitive topics of conversation, as in, "Hey Sweetie, do we have any more of that i-c-e-c-r-e-a-m left?"

I've adapted to the point where I no longer question the absurd. When Julia announced that she had a gift for me and produced a fancy new diaper/toy/utility bag, I took it in stride, although I was momentarily taken aback by the luxurious black velvety fabric, the blood-red satin interior, and the leopard-skin shoulder straps. The thing seemed a little over-the-top for toting diapers, but what do I know about fashion? Everything I've worn for the past fifteen years has come from the Salvation Army.

Then I noticed the tag, which read, "Made for you especially by Monica™."

"You're kidding," I said. Julia was laughing; it was true. This was a sample of Monica Lewinsky's latest calling: handmade designer bags. I can accept talking plastic pigs and books with free will, but Monica's Amazing Technicolor Dreambag was really stretching my tolerance for the surreal.

I expressed misgivings about her qualifications. The care instructions recommend Dry Clean Only, but why take her word for it? She hasn't exactly established a track record as a stain-removal authority. Maybe she hired a technical consultant.

Anyway, what does Monica Lewinsky know about childcare? Probably about as much as I know about shagging the President, which is to say, not much. What's next, the Kenneth Starr Yoga Video?

Emma looked on in puzzlement as Julia and I laughed ourselves silly while pondering these and other possibilities. It's going to be a while before I can explain why I won't use it. For the time being, let's just say it doesn't match my shoes.

COOKING UP EXCUSES FOR POOR HOUSEKEEPING

Myth: Homedaddy does it all. Fact: Emma spends some of her mornings at daycare.

Sorry to burst your bubble, but there are certain things I can't accomplish while a pre-schooler is running amok experimenting with new personality combinations (Little Bo Peep-meets-Mike Tyson and Martha Stewart-meets-John Belushi have both shown promising results this week).

Housecleaning is impossible. Not just washing dishes and doing laundry, but the real rubber-glove stuff like scrubbing toilets, or opening those

ancient containers of Mystery Leftovers that have been shunted to the back of the fridge. Children need the kind of love and attention you can't provide when you're genuflecting over the shower tile grout with a steel wool pad.

Hence, some daycare is in order. Which brings us to the heart of the matter. Myth: Homedaddy cleans the house while Emma is at daycare. Fact: Homedaddy does no such thing. Our house retains a look that a Beltway spin-doctor might describe as "lived-in," although others might assume the entire premises had been turned upside down and shaken.

With Emma at daycare, my normal reaction to household entropy is to start planning a dinner menu. The trick is to think of something that is just complicated enough to be successfully prepared, while leaving no time whatsoever for cleaning. If it's early in the day, and the house is in particularly bad shape, then dinner should be rather elaborate.

Yesterday I took one look at the dust-and-dog-hair tumbleweeds under the couch and was immediately inspired to poach a salmon.

Perhaps I set my sights too low, or perhaps I was too efficient at the fish counter; for whatever reason I found myself back home with time to spare. I frantically consulted a cookbook and discovered, to my relief, that it would be a nice touch to poach the salmon in homemade fish stock rather than just water and seasonings. Homemade fish stock! Now that sounded time consuming. I was headed back to the market before you could say "disinfectant antifungal scrubbing bubbles."

I took my time selecting fish bones for stock, because quality is everything, you know.

An hour or so later, with the dinner project under control, there was still the possibility I might have some time left to clean the house. Another frantic reading of the recipe yielded no further details. I tried another cookbook and hit pay-dirt. It mentioned in passing that some cooks prefer to wrap the salmon in cheesecloth before poaching, to make it easier to lift it out of the pan. Was this a necessary step? Since we had no cheesecloth on hand, the answer was a resounding Yes. Back to the market.

The cheesecloth turned out to be a good idea. The salmon was perfect. My only mistake was cooking too much of it. We'll be eating the leftovers for days.

Maybe Emma's had enough daycare this week…

LIFE OF THE POTTY

There is no aspect of childhood that is so remote, so fleeting, or so personal that some bunch of rubes somewhere are not trying to exploit it for a buck.

The interests and personalities of the entrepreneurs are reflected in their chosen specialties. There are literary-minded folks who develop and market toys to teach the alphabet, sports fans who sell games of manual dexterity, and food buffs hawking everything from fancy bibs to miniature kitchen sets.

And then there's the potty training crowd.

A web search on the phrase "potty training" turns up a variety of products designed by people who are probably trying to be helpful but who should be closely monitored nonetheless.

One company sells a "motivational chart" that looks like a board game to chronicle your child's potty progress. In a stroke of pure genius (or perhaps confusion) they suggest that you put the chart up on the refrigerator. Toddlers may be too young to appreciate this subtle bit of alimentary humor, but at least visitors to your home can keep up-to-date on your child's current level of sphincter control. This may be the best little conversation piece of all time for getting rid of unwanted guests.

There were a number of musical potty seats that play a song when a child "succeeds." Great care should be taken to ensure that the child does not make an unfortunate association between going to the toilet and making music — a phenomenon which could account for much of what is now heard on commercial radio. Generally, these devices are harmless as long as they don't play the national anthem, which could cause your little patriot to leap to his feet at an unfortunate moment, resulting in embarrassment, injury, or political alienation.

One web page claims "the most advanced training aid ever produced in the history of potty training" (note to self: write up a proposal for the History Channel). Listed among the many beneficial side effects: "Teaches Manners, Creates Sense of Humor, Promotes Positive Thinking, Great Gift Idea..."

What exactly is this miracle product, this scientific breakthrough? Ladies and Gentlemen, I present to you (trumpet fanfare) The Happy Bull's-Eye Target Sticker ... a quarter-sized toilet bowl decal featuring a smiley face and the words "Thank You." So simple, yet, so elegant.

In the name of consumer advocacy, I E-mailed this company for substantiation of the theory that urinating on a smiley face might teach manners or promote positive thinking. Expressing concerns about potential long-term side effects, I wondered what happens when a graduate of the Happy Bull's-Eye Method has a breakdown as an adult? It's enough to make you think twice about saying "Have a nice day" to a total stranger.

A company representative wrote back to pooh-pooh my concerns. Directing my attention back to the web page (how could I have missed it?) she reiterated The Happy Bull's-Eye Creed: "We honor and respect our customers."

Yep, there's no denying it, at Happy Bull's-Eye, the customer is Number One.

YES, BUT IS IT ART?

All sources of parenting advice will tell you to foster your child's creativity, which is about as helpful as being told to think good thoughts. Young children are naturally creative; the real trick is to let them express it without becoming a danger to themselves and to society at large.

Of all the visual media, Emma prefers paint for its bright colors, its ability to quickly fill large areas, and its unsurpassed mess potential. Crayons are OK, but how much trouble can you make with crayons? After all, a parent could actually leave a two-year-old alone in a room with crayons, so how exciting could they be?

I thought I had our painting routine under control the other day: newspaper on the floor, lots of spare paper on hand, and funky used clothing that I would just as soon burn as wash. I gave Emma an empty egg carton as a palette, using a teaspoon to dispense extra paint as needed.

My big mistake was to leave the spoon sitting in the egg carton. Paint, paper, eggs, spoon… and now a spoon with paint on it! A visual pun on the relationship between art and food; how very droll! Not to be outdone, Emma picked it up and pantomimed taking a bite, just to test the waters. My reaction was immediate and unequivocal: "No! No eating paint."

I admit, she wasn't actually eating the paint, she was only pretending to eat it, but little kids are not allowed to make jokes about eating paint any more than smartass grown-ups are allowed to joke about bombs while having a carry-on bag searched.

Emma made another move toward her mouth with the spoon, watching me closely. I countered with a nifty little piece of body English meant to convey the complex notion of "Don't make me come over there," but all it did was raise the stakes. Brinksmanship is not a useful negotiating strategy with a two-year-old. The spoon shot into her mouth.

Of course it was non-toxic paint, but cause for swift intervention nonetheless. I wrestled the spoon from her hand and carried her into another room. I tried to defuse her mounting panic by calmly explaining

RIGHT   WRONG

that she was not in trouble, but that we had to talk about something. I even told her that she could keep painting when we were done talking, but it was no use. Kids know when they are getting a lecture no matter how you dress it up, and they tend to tune it out. I kept it simple: No... eating... paint... EVER!

After this little chat, Emma did not want to resume painting, which made me feel the collective guilt from all those parenting articles warning me not to stifle my child's creative spirit. When I brought home some new paints a few days later, I was relieved when she went at it with the old gusto, and even more so when she didn't call for her spoon.

MEASURING UP TO MARTHA

There is nothing like reading a Martha Stewart publication to remind a Homedaddy that in terms of essential homemaking skills such as restoring authentic Colonial Era spittoons or using only fresh-picked cranberries from the private bog on one's own property for Holiday Dressing, he is nothing but a stone failure.

I may have had delusions about completing household projects when I first became a Homedaddy, but after two years of childcare, I consider it a personal triumph if everyone has clean underwear and the garbage cans are brought back from the curb at some point during the week.

Not content to make the average homemaker feel like a total loser, Martha Stewart has now released a "Special Baby Issue." Among the clinically detailed articles about decorating diaper pails with something called "ticking," I spotted the "Ask Martha" feature where readers send in queries about life at home with a baby. For the first time, I thought, "Aha, she can't tell me anything I don't know." As a test, I lifted her readers' questions word for word and answered them myself, just to see what I could do.

MARTHA

Q: *How can I be sure that my baby's crib is as safe as possible?*
A: *Personally, I think you worry too much, but if you think your baby's crib is in danger you should secure it with a heavy-duty bike lock. If you live in a really terrible neighborhood you can purchase an inexpensive crib alarm system or simply bolt the crib to the house foundation.*

Q: *How do we announce that we have adopted a baby?*
A: *That all depends on your station in life. If you are a major Hollywood type then a full page announcement in Variety plus a few billboards on Sunset are appropriate. Otherwise, a simple battery-powered megaphone should do the trick.*

Q: *Is it all right for a baby to be taken out to a restaurant?*
A: *Yes, as long as you tell the baby's parents where you are going and when you'll be back. You should also be prepared to pick up the tab; babies are notoriously old-fashioned.*

Q: *What are the pros and cons of cloth and disposable diapers?*
A: *On the pro side, diapers offer the necessary protection for furniture, bedding, and clothing. The downside is that most babies prefer to be naked and will demonstrate their dislike for diapers in the most graphic way imaginable.*

Q: *Should I prepare my pets for my baby?*
A: *Heavens, no. The baby won't be ready for solid food for a few more months yet.*

That went rather well, don't you think? Maybe I'll venture into the craft arena while I'm at it. If Martha can do it, why can't I? Tune in next week and I'll tell you how to take the carcass from the Thanksgiving turkey, kiln-dry it, paint it with gold leaf, and turn it upside down to fashion a whimsically festive holiday potty seat.

RIDE 'EM HOMEDADDY

When Julia first became pregnant about three years ago, we considered keeping both jobs and hiring a full-time nanny, but we quickly rejected this plan on financial as well as emotional grounds. Since Julia loved her work and was also earning the lion's share, it was my job that went on the block.

I bailed out of my low-paying, stress-filled job in a hot second. Easiest decision I've ever made. Before you could say "cradle cap," I became a Emma's full-time parent amid so much support and admiration, you'd think I had volunteered for a suicide mission, rather than something that women have been doing forever with no fanfare and hardly any thanks.

Childcare has traditionally been considered "women's work." Now that men are getting involved, full-time parenting will probably be legitimized as a respectable vocation, if not a noble pursuit. If enough men do it, you can expect it to become a full-fledged Sport, complete with leagues, playoffs, and beer commercials.

ESPN2 will have to bump the "Huge Men With Suspicious Chromosomes Tossing Farm Implements" competition to clear the schedule for the Homedaddy Finals. Full-time fathers from around the world will compete in various categories as they vie for the title of Grand Champion Homedaddy... and the honor of donning the coveted Master's Apron, with its colorful fingerpaint-and-vomit motif designed by Leroy Neiman.

The Newborn Division events will include Sleep Deprivation and Birth Announcement Addressing (points deducted for cross-outs, wasted envelopes, and returned mail). The Infant Division will feature Freestyle Sleep Induction, Speed Burping, and Silly Noises (judged on artistic merit ... look out for those tough, humorless Eastern European judges!). Homedaddies in the Stock Baby Division will accumulate point totals in various Stroller Racing events before advancing to the Nike/VISA/Fisher Price Tee Shirt Shootout in which contestants attempt to pull a tee shirt with a pathetically undersized neck opening over a one-year-old's head in under eight seconds. Causing the baby to cry results in a disqualification, or "no time."

Featuring the strongest, fastest, and most cunning children, the Toddler Division will draw the biggest crowds and the highest advertising rates. In the Furniture Race, a timed event, a chair, a sofa, and a coffee table will be placed in a triangular formation in the arena. The Homedaddy, carrying a toothbrush in one hand, must chase the toddler around all three pieces of furniture in a cloverleaf pattern. Five seconds will be added to his time if anything is knocked over, and barking a shin on the coffee table will result in immediate disqualification.

With elements of calf roping, steer wrestling, and bareback riding, the Bedtime Sprint will be the main event. As the official timer sounds a bell to signify bedtime, a naked toddler will be given a three-second head start toward the front door. Giving chase through an obstacle course of wheeled toys, the Homedaddy must catch the child from behind, carry him back into the house, wrestle him to the ground, and prepare him for bed with the fresh diaper he carries in his teeth. When the diaper is secure, the Homedaddy will throw his hands in the air as a signal to the flag judge.

Childcare is a contact sport; there are bound to be tantrums and boo-boos. In a situation gone bad, the Clowndaddies will jump in to cheer up the baby with crowd-pleasing antics, while providing a safe escape for the Homedaddy in trouble.

The popularity of this sport will surpass everyone's wildest expectations, and it won't be long before Homedaddy events are included in the Olympics. Who knows? Even women may eventually be allowed to compete.

WHEN THEY DON'T WIN IT'S A SHAME

I recently moonlighted once again as an umpire for Little League® Baseball, and although it was my first such outing in well over a year, I figured that being a Homedaddy would be pretty good mental conditioning. Already entrenched in the authoritarian mind set, I strode onto the field wearing my "Throw-that-sippy-cup-one-more-time-and-I'll-take-it-away" face. True, these kids were ten-to-twelve-year-olds, but I knew my attitude would take them back to a time of hard lessons and frontier justice.

Kids at this age are far more receptive to law and order than your stock toddler, who responds to authority about as well as a werewolf. These kids were remarkably well-behaved compared to what I am used to, and after the first inning I was really starting to enjoy saying "Stee-rike" without feeling compelled to follow up with "Because I said so" by way of explanation.

Umpiring and parenting have much in common. I noticed that as long as I wasn't needed, people thought I was doing a great job. For the first few innings, all the strikes were being thrown right down the middle, all base runners were thrown out by at least two steps, all fly balls were caught cleanly, and I had fans aplenty. "Good call, Blue!" bellowed one parent, after I raised my fist in the air to signal a swing-and-miss third strike.

I have had the same experience as a parent. When Emma is in a particularly sweet mood, entertaining herself and those around her in a checkout line, for example, I have had perfect strangers offer compliments on my relaxed, yet effective parenting style. I smile and nod my thanks, wondering what this person would have thought of the red-faced, milk-throwing tantrum that delayed the trip to the market by two hours.

The reverse also holds true, which is to say that when the game starts to get out of hand, the umpire (or parent, as the case may be) is likely to catch the blame. They love you when things are clear-cut, but when it is time to call a close one, you know for a fact that half of the people present are going to think you are stupid, blind, corrupt, and drunk with power, if not with something else.

It's the same story at home. Emma starts to clamor for dessert before finishing dinner. I say, "Three more bites of broccoli and then you can have some dessert." She then eats two bites of broccoli, and after pushing the third one around the plate for a minute, announces "All done!" It all comes down to a judgement call. Will she reach base safely and get her treat, or will she be called out at the plate?

As an umpire, or as a Homedaddy, one must remember that it isn't a popularity contest; you have to call 'em like you see 'em. At game's end I got many dirty looks from the losers, but at least I didn't have to take them all home and make them eat their vegetables.

STICKERS AND OTHER BRIBES

A few chapters ago I reviewed a potty training product called the "Happy Bull's-Eye Target Sticker." Employing responsible investigative journalistic technique (I wrote a prank E-mail to the company, which they actually answered), I was able to successfully de-bunk some of their misleading marketing claims. Unfortunately, a small handful of readers misinterpreted the column as a wholesale dismissal of the value of stickers to the Toddler Experience. I shall respond to these scurrilous charges in the time-honored fashion, by suggesting that these people grow a brain.

Any successful Toddler Management scheme must sooner or later make use of delayed gratification, known in corporate circles as Carrot-And-Stick. Many parents typically offer sweets as rewards, although I have found this to be unsuitable, since most children will drop everything in order to rapidly devour the goodie, thereby returning herself and the parent to Square One. It's a dead-end scenario prone to rapid escalation and a zero-sum outcome.

Television, another traditional bonus, is likewise not supported by Homedaddy Laboratories® because of its propensity for candy advertising, as well as it's potential to expose your child to inappropriate themes like sex, violence, and politics.

Stickers, on the other hand, represent breakthrough technology in the field of Toddler Management. They are cheap and plentiful; and from the child's perspective, highly desirable.

It is hard to account for the near-mystical attraction stickers hold for little kids. The wide diversity of subjects depicted seems to suggest that the particular image is not as important as the very fact of sticker-ness. As an experiment, cut two identical shapes from a piece of colored paper, coat the back of one with a glue stick, and offer them both to your child. Within moments, the simple colored shape will be discarded in favor of the adhesive-enabled version, which will be immediately elevated to the status of a holy object.

In the toddler's perpetual battle against gravity, a sticker, which adheres effortlessly to vertical or even overhanging surfaces, must be a very powerful object. Perhaps it is this ability defy the laws of the natural universe which makes stickers so attractive.

We have used them as effective encouragement for numerous activities, from finishing dinner to brushing teeth. We've also used stickers for potty training, but only in their traditional role as incentives. With all due respect to the Happy Bull's-Eye Target Sticker company, it is my opinion that the use of stickers as urination targets tends to depreciate their value as rewards for other positive behaviors.

For several months now we have allowed Emma to put a sticker on her potty seat each time she uses it, with the result that it is now totally covered. I imagine that the first time she sees an Ohio State football game on TV she'll take one look at the quarterback's sticker-covered helmet and draw some definite conclusions about his bathroom skills.

Coming soon: Tips and tricks for cleaning the stickers off a potty seat with a common sandblaster.

THE PRICE OF HIGH FASHION

Babies never fail to invoke deep feelings of love and tenderness, especially among advertisers, for whom the prospect of taking your money warms the heart like a cup of steaming cocoa prepared by faceless, low-wage servants working quietly and efficiently behind closed doors.

When a Homedaddy reads one of the many slick parenting magazines, he may initially feel left out by the unmistakably feminine orientation of the color scheme, the selection of typefaces, and especially the advertising. This must be what women baseball fans feel like between innings as they suffer through one stud-fantasy razor blade commercial after another.

The new-parent market, which is really the new-mother market, is such a gold mine that clothing giant The Gap has a separate entity called babyGap which seems to be single-handedly funding most of these magazines with their muti-page advertising spreads.

I can tell right away that I am not the target audience. Leafing through page after page of focus group-approved pastel color combinations, I can almost hear the bullets of market research whiz past my head and ricochet off towards another demographic. An innocent bystander, I proceed with caution.

Wandering through the soft-sell landscapes, I marvel at the various offerings. Cashmere pants, $75. Mohair cardigan, $58, with optional mohair "shell," $48. Something called a cashmere "shrug" for $78 that looks like the top half of a sweater. You've got to be kidding. You want me to put $75 cashmere pants on a creature whose defining feature is a total lack of bowel control? Even if constant vigilance keeps the garment from becoming a dry cleaner's nightmare, the child's growth will render it obsolete in six weeks.

I have nothing against the babyGap line of clothing, or against fancy baby clothes in general. In her own baby Gap duds, Emma is as cute as any old baby model in some parenting magazine. We find the clothes in our local thrift stores for about 79 cents a pop. I get the dual satisfaction of supporting a good cause and still being a cheapskate. Emma gets to be a fashion plate, and then I can take a philosophical view when she decorates her "silk resort capri pants" with marker pens.

I do not recommend that everyone get their baby clothes at thrift stores. Someone has to buy them new in order to feed my supply line. Besides, only strong retail sales can support the magazine layouts, which allow me to see the actual retail prices... not just so I can feel smart and superior, but also because it helps me figure out how much to deduct as charity when I donate them back again after Emma outgrows them.

I needn't worry; connoisseurs of "retail therapy" will continue to insist on the real thing. Thrift stores fail to deliver that special euphoria of spending, described by some as an "out-of-money experience." It is a brief but intense high that gives way to an inevitable crash, during which the shopper is suddenly able to comprehend the difference between the advertised image and the actual piece of merchandise. That's probably why they call it The Gap.

BARF, BEARS, AND BOULDERS

According to auto manufacturers and oil companies, the sheer pleasure of shoehorning everyone into the car for a family vacation ranks as the number one reason for having children. They also claim that inhaling directly from your vehicle's tailpipe is good for you.

Precautions must be taken to avoid the natural enemy of family travel: motion sickness, the perils of which are well known to me. As a child I would get queasy when the car was still backing out of the driveway. Any trip longer than ten minutes was touch-and-go, and winding roads were the kiss of death. Car-sickness was a central theme of childhood; my Hot Wheels set even had a little pull-out area where you could stop the toy car and heave till you see stars while your siblings laugh themselves into next week.

Last weekend we hit the road for Yosemite National Park, a mere jaunt at five hours. The laboratory-tested "bedtime departure" technique worked rather well initially but then failed during the final hour of twisting mountain road, at which point Emma snapped awake and demanded that books be read to her. Motion-sensitivity is exacerbated by riding in the back seat or by reading; to attempt both at once is asking for trouble. Factor in the thousandth reading of *The Runaway Bunny* and you have a procedure NASA could use for astronaut conditioning.

Once within the park boundaries we encountered lots of anti-bear propaganda, since bears are apparently a very real hazard. We saw a poster with a photograph that looks like the "after" shot of a highway wreck pried open with the Jaws of Life, but which was actually a parked car casually swatted open by a condominium-sized bear who happened to spy an ice chest on the seat.

Thusly terrified, I set out to clean our car's interior for the first time in years, but I got discouraged and gave up when I realized there are enough goldfish cracker crumbs in the carpets and upholstery to sustain a family of bears for an entire summer.

The concern over bears confused Emma, who still knows them as fuzzy, cuddly Stewards of Dreamland, rather than gigantic, thundering killing machines that would just as soon disembowel you as look at you. They say that in case of a bear "encounter" you are supposed to play dead, but I figure this is only because you might as well get used to the idea.

In Yosemite Valley you still stand a better chance of being run over by a tour bus than ever seeing a bear, which is another reason to take a hike besides to impress your children. In her developing capacity for understatement, Emma gazed up at the sheer 3000-foot granite rise of El Capitan and muttered "Big rock."

Overall, she took a liking to the place. Between the spectacular sights and our constant repetition of the name "Yosemite," she seems to have assumed a measure of ownership, and, for the time being, refers to it as MY-semite.

SIMON SAYS WRITE YOUR COLUMN

Sooner or later, defiant behavior presents a knotty problem for parents, except for those brutal disciplinarians for whom the course of action is clear, and whose children may eventually aspire to great success pitching their Repressed Memory Syndrome books on the Oprah Winfrey show. The task of the modern parent is to find new ways to exert authority and establish constructive routines without being a total jerk.

Mealtimes and dental hygiene are classic areas of difficulty. Some toddlers would no sooner eat their corn than prepare a tax return, while others are about as receptive to having their teeth brushed as having their fingernails trimmed with a chain saw. In either case, a parent can easily exhaust his arsenal of cajoling, begging, and demanding with little or no effect, a deeply frustrating result in light of prevailing societal expectations. Dental authorities suggest that tooth and gum cleaning begin in infancy, and that Baby's teeth be flossed as soon as two teeth appear next to each other, although personally, I can't imagine any practical use for dental floss unless you use it to tie the child down while you brush his teeth.

Many parents, lacking the strength to carry on, have turned to a Higher Power for help. Adherents to this lifestyle claim miraculous results, noting that even very young children are able to grasp the essence of an unseen being more powerful than parents, a presence so strong that it has the ability to eclipse the toddler's snowballing ego. In accordance with tradition handed down over generations, this guiding force may be invoked through a simple ritual in which the parent takes a moment to clear away all negative thought before gazing lovingly and gently into the child's eyes and speaking the words, "Simon Says."

Celia Phate, president and sole member of NUTS (Nation Under the Teachings of Simon) claims that children as young as two days can benefit greatly from the knowledge that "Simon is at the controls of the universe," and that toddlers, especially, are quick to accept the benevolent messages embedded in simple commands, such as "Simon Says eat your corn."

Other experts are alarmed by the proliferation of Simon Says groups, and some have gone so far as to identify it as a cult. SimonWatch, a public advocacy group, provides guidelines to determine if your spouse or child is participating in a Simon Says cult: Has Simon Says taken control of your child's life, determining what to eat and wear, or when to sleep or bathe? Has Simon become authoritarian in his power structure? Is there an ethical double standard? Have you noticed that Simon never brushes his teeth or eats his corn, although he commands it of his followers? Does your child not question what "Simon Says?"

As usual, the Homedaddy Institute® discounts extremist reports on both sides of the issue, and recommends that you eat your own corn before browbeating your child. If you are disturbed by the information presented in this article, well… Simon Says get a life.

LITTLE WHITE LIES

As a society, we set standards for our children which adults are not required to meet. Volumes have been written about teaching children to share; it's an industry already. You take your kid to the park with his pail and shovel set, and while you're on the swings, some other kid waddles up and starts to play with the shovel. When your kid starts to whine, he gets a lecture about sharing.

Meanwhile, if someone so much as repositions a ceramic gnome in your front yard, you call the police to report vandalism. Grown-ups generally do not share their toys the same way we ask our children to share theirs. Bear in mind that a child might own one pail and shovel set during his entire early childhood. The experience in the park might be the equivalent of a total stranger hopping into your car to go run an errand, while you stand there in the parking lot whining in protest.

No issue exemplifies this double standard better than lying. On an individual, personal basis, we hate being lied to; yet our popular culture is defined by fantasy, exaggeration, hubris, and plain old bull-product.

Many people deny this fact while others just resign themselves to being powerless over it. After all, what are you going to do, phone your Senators and tell them if they don't knock it off right now you'll send them to bed with no dessert? Write a letter to a car maker telling them that if you see one more commercial suggesting that their car can bestow sexual powers, you'll take away their crayons?

Out of frustration, ignorance, or hope, many of us turn our attention toward our kids. A featured article in a recent issue of a national parenting magazine is entitled "Why Kids Lie," as if there is some great mystery involved here. Amid much hand-wringing, the article mentions lots of clinical stuff about toddlers being in the early stages of determining what's real and make-believe, and having a hard time distinguishing their dreams from reality, while ignoring the fact that adult hustlers of every stripe are making a living off their lies.

I'm not saying that popular culture causes children to become liars. As the article says, lying comes naturally to little kids. They lie their diapers off. They'll say anything to get out of eating some nutritious food or brushing their teeth, or even just for the heck of it. Just today, Emma told me there was a monster on her shoe with two noses, even though she didn't stand to gain anything, so far as I could tell.

There is no cause for alarm about small children telling lies. It can all be handled in the time-honored fashion, by imparting the wisdom of the ages through one-on-one story telling. If your child is getting carried away with lying, tell him the story of *The Boy Who Cried Wolf.* Just to be on the safe side, though, you might wait a few years before admitting that it isn't a true story.

SHARE THE ROD AND SOIL THE CHILD

To all you parents who bring your kids to the park and then relax while your chip-off-the-old-block runs amok in the play area: Please invest the dollar ninety eight in a plastic pail-and-shovel set, so that your little search-and-destroy unit will not be overcome with greed and envy at the sight of Emma's pail and shovel, and therefore will not feel compelled to seize them by force.

Honestly, you'd think these kids never saw a pail and shovel before, or that the idea of actually bringing them to a large sand-filled play area was somehow revolutionary.

The other day Emma and I were sitting there making sand cakes, when a little guy about her age careened over, and, surveying the scene, declared everything in his field of vision as his own personal property by uttering the magic word "Guh." He then demonstrated the New Order by yanking Emma's shovel out of her hand and whacking her with it.

OK, maybe he didn't really whack her; maybe he got excited with the shovel in his hand and was making an exuberant gesture with an unfortunate result. You have to give these little ones the benefit of the doubt.

The whole time, Emma is giving me that Look, the one that says, "You told me to share so I am sharing, and now I have been whacked on the head, so am I missing something or are you a total idiot?"

Then the parent arrives on the scene, and guess what? It's another dad! Full-timer or just slumming, I can't tell. He apologizes profusely (although not sufficiently, in my book) and speaks for his son, asking if they can share our toys. Emma is furiously shaking her head like she's in a cloud of gnats but I speak for her and say "Sure."

Then she really gives me the Look.

The little boy sits down next to her and scoops some sand with the shovel, and for a split second I enjoy the delusion that these kids will just play. But no, he suffers from SCD, Sand Control Disorder, which causes him to jerk suddenly as if he had been stung by a wasp (no such luck) and fling the sand at the nearest human face, which would be Emma's.

Sand in the eyes, sand in the mouth… it wasn't a good situation. And this dad is droning on in his best Mister Rogers voice about playing nice, while the kid, with that horrible gleam in his eye, is already digging another load and taking aim.

Since his dad wasn't going to intervene, I put my hand on the shovel (you have to be mindful of putting your hands on other people's kids) and said something profound like "Hey, man…" The other dad took the hint and scooped his kid up to go have a Talk.

Since then, when we head for the park, Emma looks me in the eye and intones, "I WON'T share my toys." I'm trying to restore her faith in humankind, but I know better than to rush it.

MOSQUITO NETWORKING

During the recent streak of hot weather, driven to desperate measures by our lack of air conditioning, we spent a few nights with the windows thrown wide open. This total disregard for the consequences led to the inadvertent discovery of a simple but effective mosquito control plan, which is to keep a small, defenseless child sleeping nearby.

Mosquitoes tend to breed in bodies of standing water around one's property, or perhaps in my case, among the dirty dishes in the sink. And why, you might ask, do I not have screens on the windows? OK, it is a good question, I'll grant you that; let's just say it is on my list of things to do. After this week it has moved up a couple of notches.

Emma collected five or six bites on her cheeks that quickly swelled to dramatic proportions. Mosquito bites, as we all know, do not hurt, but boy, do they itch, and this is where things get tricky.

How, exactly, is one to convince a two-year-old not to scratch at her mosquito bites? One technique recommended by expert geeks who live alone with no children is to sit down with your child and slowly and calmly explain what mosquitoes are, how and why they bite, and the chemical reactions that take place in the skin which cause the irritation. The trick is to maintain eye contact and continue talking for three or four days until the swelling goes down.

If this doesn't work, you can try calamine lotion, which soothes the itch but creates an attractive pink crust which will make her look like the loser in a paintball war. While it seems to control the itching, it is also apparently irresistible to the touch, and functions as a "warm up" layer to work on before she gets down to her actual skin. At this point most parents resort to the time-honored and highly ineffective technique of nagging the child every few seconds to stop scratching at the bites.

Parents of the truly incorrigible picker may want to try out one of those white plastic cone-collars used to prevent dogs from chewing on themselves. Although they are undoubtedly a fashion faux pas (George Jetson does Shakespeare), they do get the job done. Even if your child looks like she is wearing a satellite dish, at least she'll be getting all the premium channels at a fraction of the cost of cable TV.

Fearing the judgement of friends and neighbors, I stuck with traditional methods, but despite my constant refrain of "Don't pick at it," the condition of Emma's mosquito bites deteriorated to the point that she appeared to be disguised as a piece of beef jerky.

Everyone has a method to stop a kid from scratching mosquito bites. The American Psychiatric Association endorses the use of straitjackets, The Sierra Club suggests wool mittens, and The International Pharmaceutical Manufacturers propose an array of behavior-altering drugs. The Painters and Plasterers Union, taking their traditional stance against scabs, recommends a long lasting, spray-on stucco finish.

I think I'll try window screens.

LAND OF THE GIANTS

We had already taken Emma to see two major league baseball games at The-Ballpark-Formerly-Known-As-Candlestick, so during this week's visit to San Francisco, we decided to take in a game at Pacific Bell Park, the new home of the Giants.

The last time Emma had been to a game was a year ago at one year of age; she spent most of the time on our laps and even slept through the late innings. Now that she is able to locomote and demand junk food under her

own power, I had to consider the possibility of buying an extra ticket. Not necessary, according to the ticket office, as long as she can sit on your lap during the game without disturbing the fans in front of her.

I knew she wouldn't stay on our laps, but I also knew she wouldn't stay in a seat either, so I heeded my Inner Cheapskate and skipped the third ticket. She was constantly on the go after the first inning, and the people in front of us would have never known she was there if not for a negligible amount of soda dribbled down the back of their necks.

Tip for parents: Don't bother buying good seats. It makes sense with an infant, but a toddler keeps you too busy for serious spectating. While I thoroughly enjoyed the ambience, I was only dimly aware that there was a game in progress. Buy cheap seats; you'll need the extra money for food, drinks, and souvenirs. The last time I paid six-fifty for a beer there were six of them, and they came in a handy little cardboard carrying case.

Being surrounded by thousands of people gorging themselves on all manner of junk food can be a powerful experience in the life of a toddler. Here's another tip: Get a nutritious meal down the hatch before coming to the game; it's a long night and the temptations are many. Emma went right to the big guns, calling for ice cream, and it took two innings to plea-bargain her down to lemonade.

We were in the clear for another inning till the vendor came down the steps, bellowing "Ice cream! Getcha ice cream right here!" Once again, parental authority eroded by social excess. Thanks a lot, buddy.

I browsed the stadium gift shop, which was itself large enough to house a couple of minor league teams. They even have a section just for babies, where I found an official Giants sippy cup, autographed by first baseman J.T. Snow, who is, mysteriously, the only player to endorse such an item. While other athletes are fooling around with soft drink and shoe endorsements, Snow has established himself as The Man in the sippy cup industry. At eleven dollars, it was the bargain of the day.

I give the new ballpark high marks, overall. I just think it would be better if they could train the ice cream vendors to yell: "I-C-E C-R-E-A-M! Getcha I-C-E C-R-E-A-M here!"

FATHER'S DAY, SHMATHER'S DAY

Most of our holidays are based on war, religion, or politics. Father's Day, on the other hand, is basically a national effort to boost second-quarter retail sales.

Besides supporting the necktie and greeting card industries, Father's Day also provides Moms and kids the chance to offset some of the guilt accumulated by treating Dad like a doormat during the other 364 days of the year. For those fathers who are basically absent, emotionally or otherwise, the copious holiday propaganda serves to refresh the myth that, yes, they play crucial roles in providing a stable family unit and a loving, nurturing environment for little what's-his-name.

Father's Day is allegedly the single busiest day for long-distance telephone calls, which means that many people feel obligated to phone their fathers on that pre-arranged special day. Then, after that brief call, about as spontaneous and heartfelt as a press conference, they're off the hook for a while.

This doesn't stop advertisers, TV programmers, and politicians from milking it for all its worth, publicly endorsing Father's Day as a symbol for the long-lost goodness of family life. Not to be outdone, the State of Oregon (motto: Bob Packwood's still gone... we promise!) even issued a proclamation in 1998 declaring June 21-28 to be Fatherhood Week.

The proclamation is full of serious words like "witnesseth" and "whereas," and it grapples with many hard-hitting facts such as: "Fathers play a unique role in the lives of our children," and "Healthy and socially developed children are vital to the interest and future of Oregon." Of course this was all just idle talk until the governor, "in witness whereof, hereunder set his hand and caused the great seal to be affixed," with the inevitable result that fathers all over Oregon are snapping to attention and remarking, "Hey, I'm feeling really mindful of the importance of my role in society!"

This Homedaddy® doesn't really need Father's Day, let alone Fatherhood Week. I get to be at home with Emma every day, which provides me with all the recognition I need. I'm already in charge of all the food, so if I crave a special meal, I go ahead and cook it a couple of times a week. Gifts are always nice, but I haven't needed a tie since I went to my last funeral and I'm in no hurry for the next one.

For the traditional dad who spends the majority of his time out of the house, a day lounging in the living room might be just the ticket. If, on the other hand, you already spend nearly all of your time in the house, you might prefer to go somewhere alone on your special day, even if that's not exactly in keeping with the spirit of things.

If I really wanted to be King of the House, I'd force Emma to call me "Your Majesty," to make crowns for me out of construction paper and glitter, and to taste all of my food before I put it to my lips. If I so desired, I could get the royal treatment every day… and probably wind up as one of the dads who get their one call a year.

Afterword / Preface to the next Homedaddy collection

Some friends, taking note of my casual comments recently about another baby on the way, may wonder why I haven't brought it up again. Aside from a few cryptic statements here and there, I seem to have been strangely silent on this topic.

In response to the initial shock of confirmed pregnancy, my endocrine system apparently dumped a few quarts of RAH, Reality Avoidance Hormone, into my bloodstream. This precipitated a condition known as Gestational Abstraction, during which I was able to accept the pregnancy as an intellectual concept while remaining oblivious to it as a rapidly-approaching physical reality. By focusing on the minute details of the daily household routine, I was able to remain only dimly aware of, and unconsciously resistant to, the fact that things are about to change dramatically. Again.

Last week, my stalled-out sense of time finally began to collapse in on itself, and the big day (or night) loomed suddenly closer, bringing to mind one of my favorite bumper stickers: "Warning: dates on calendar are closer than they appear." This quantum leap of awareness was catalyzed by two events: The first was the official "home visit" by the midwife's assistant, normally scheduled a few weeks before the due date. The second was the simple act of making the bed, but this time with the custom addition of a rubber mattress cover.

That's right, you heard me. I said midwife. And rubber mattress cover.

Any lingering doubts I may have once had about home birth were obliterated when Emma was born, wonderfully, smoothly, and peacefully, at home, under the superb direction of our midwives. Not that we're neo-Luddites, mind you. We've had amniocentesis and sonograms, and we already know that another daughter is coming.

Clearly, this isn't the place to debate the relative merits of home versus hospital birth. If you are interested, you can educate yourself with the abundance of available information. Although Julia, Emma, and I heartily endorse home birth, it isn't for everyone in this day and age. I would venture to say that if the very idea of a rubber mattress cover pushes the limits of your personal comfort zone, this activity may not be for you.

Our morning with the midwife's assistant was spent discussing medical supplies, emergency phone numbers, and care for Emma, since she is too young, in our opinion, to be present for the main event. Somewhere during this meeting, my body's supply of RAH suddenly dried up, and the delivery date made remarkable forward progress in my mind's calendar of events. No longer a mere abstraction, it had suddenly become a concrete physical reality.

I suppose that the act of putting a rubber mattress cover on the bed did enhance this effect. It is difficult to ignore the ramifications of such an activity.

All of a sudden, I feel like I am ready. The reality has hit me like a ton of bricks, or at least like eight pounds two ounces (Emma's birth weight). For the past few days I have been bug-eyed and sleepless. No doubt, it's just nature's way of getting me prepared for the days and nights to come.